You Carry the Heavy Stuff

———

by
Esther Bradley-DeTally

YOU CARRY THE HEAVY STUFF
Copyright © 2009 by Esther Bradley-DeTally
First Edition

Cover illustration by Melissa Suber
Back cover photo by Violetta Zein

All rights reserved. No part of this publication shall be reproduced, stored in a retrieval system, or transmitted by any means without the prior permission of the author.

ISBN 978-0-557-20933-0

Lulu Press, Inc.
http://www.lulu.com
3101 Hillsborough St.
Raleigh, North Carolina 27607
United States

For Lillian (Sue) Schreiber
January 28, 1924—December 2, 2007

This book is dedicated to Lillian Schreiber, known to all as "Sue," a flame of love and solace to me and so many others. Sue honed quietude and the art of listening to an art form.

Contents

Acknowledgments 9
Preface 11
Where I'm From, Where I Am Now, Where I Want to Be 13
Energy Displaced — Breaking Coverage 17
Kingdom By the Sea, a Modern Tale 18
Split Decision (Spring 1983) (for Tillie Olson) 20
Dick Hart 22
History of Language 24
Writing Soup (for Jack Grapes) 26
Chiaroscuro 28
Functional Smunctional 30
Once More 35
Elizabeth Farnsworth, Where Are You? Jamestown, New
    York (1998) 37
Statement of Purpose (Applying for a Grant) — (Constance
    Saltonstall, Where Are You?) Jamestown, New York
    (February 1999) 39
Getting a Lifestyle 41
Peking Noodle Company Saves the Day (January 1997) 45
The Street at 8 a.m. 47
Late Shift at the Poem Factory (for Jeff Utter, our Interfaith
    Angel, on the occasion of his 60th birthday) 49
You Carry the Heavy Stuff 51
Miss Halloran 53
Before the Golden Age 55
Road Kill 56
Children of the Stolen Ones (for Gloria Haithman —
    December 2, 2004) 57
Skin Color 60
Seeing *Syriana* 61

On the Page	63
It's Still the Same Old Story	64
Language After the 100 Year War	66
Global Soup Recipe	68
Eating Chocolate at Night	70
Being Safe	72
Esther's Narrow Straits	75
Mirror Image	77
For Liz, a Remembrance of Things Past—First Bout of Cancer (April 2006)	79
Invisible Traveler	82
Am I There Yet?	83
Waiting For Bad News—Second Bout of Cancer	85
Being on Watch—Second Bout With Cancer (Spring 2007)	88
Penciling In July 2007	91
Unbroken Line (June 2007)	93
Pieces of Soul (June 18, 2007)	95
The Color of Death	97
Horse Piss and Rotted Straw	99
Read and Sung	101
Having My Druthers	102
Packing for the Future	104
The Language of God	107
Pilgrimage—Bahá'í Shrines (March 2007)	110
Halo Moon Meets HyperPhysics over Falafel at the Mercaz	112
We All Fall Down	114
Witness	115
Taking the Voice for a Walk (Spring, 2005)	116
Why I Write (July 2007)	118
Beyond the Fringe	120
Sometimes	123

Writer's Block 124
Mercury Rises 125
Writing Weakness 126
About the Author 129

Acknowledgments

A mountain of gratitude to Steve Pulley who nudged me to publish. Steve is always a friend, writer, CHPercolator colleague, and an endless source of advice. Thanks to Mim Gottschalk's and Mandana Tarr's editing. Neda and John Amir-Abbassi came to town soon enough to read the almost done draft, and thanks to Tom Keedy, who said, "I'll read your book if you write in complete sentences." Gratitude and love to Roberta Dowell, Donna Starr and ruie Mullins, who read the early drafts; blessings upon Amelia Pawlak, who roared with laughter at some of these stories; and Rodney Vance, a fellow writer, who constantly supported. I probably have missed mention of incredible helpers along the way, so this is for all those I love, too many, too varied, and too incredible to encompass within the vehicle of mere words.

Thanks to my mother, Mary Keliher Bradley, who taught me to read and led me down the insatiable path of words. Jack Grapes' writing workshops were catalysts, as was a summer session at Chautauqua with Marjorie Agosín, as was the writing group on Yahoo's Internet writers' group, Coffee House for Writers Percolator, as well as my own teaching of the writing process. We all have something to say.

Bill, my husband, provides a constant, always forever type of foundation for which I will feel eternal gratitude. And, Esther, don't forget Ralph Schreiber, dear buddy writer and valiant husband to Sue. Finally, to the anonymous amongst us. It isn't what we do that matters. It is what we do with what we have, and I have been privileged to see nobility on a constant daily basis. This is for those who cannot speak.

Preface

Reader, *You Carry the Heavy Stuff* started out as an attempt to show various writing modes and maybe how I grew as an old gal. It evolved into musings, observances, and just plain chat stuff about things that make up my fabric of life: writing, racial justice, relationships with mother-in-law, a twin, working in law firms, health issues, spiritual concerns, and a side view of war, peace, and confusions of the day

The point? The point of this book, *You Carry the Heavy Stuff,* is that I've participated in a lot of different ways to write: the University of Irvine's writing program trickled down into fiction writing with Oakley Hall, master of the novel, and beyond this attending more than one workshop with Jack Grapes in Los Angeles. Reader, I think Jack Grapes is the Pied Piper and Daddy of all workshop leaders. That's not all, reader: I've taken education classes, participated in Teaching Writing the Natural Way, gone to UCLA writing workshops, and all that O-frabjous-joy type of thing, but I haven't written an essay on the tip of a match yet.

These last few years, I have been in a group called CHPercolator at Yahoo because my friend Steve Pulley, down the street and across the way, said, "Esther you've got to do this; belong to our computer group, which consists of writers from all around the world, who only encourage."

To tell the truth reader, I was a bit snobby about it. I was in the midst of a class with Jack Grapes where I was roaring to the moon, and thought, why? But one day after finishing Jack's stuff, I registered with the writing group. Be still my heart, reader. I have written crappola and O-frabjous-day stuff, and it all sort of collected on the computer. I had written a book about living in Russia, *Without a Net: a Sojourn in Rus-*

sia, before all this, before Jack, before CHPerc, but not before carrying heavy stuff.

The working title for this book was *Writing on the Fly*, but then along came a spider—no, not really—but along came the idea: *You Carry The Heavy Stuff*, and that's what our multi-themed lives are about. Sometimes we carry stuff, sometimes others carry stuff for us, but it's all about moving through. Best wishes to all who travel through these pages.

Esther Bradley-DeTally
Pasadena, November 2009

Where I'm From, Where I Am Now, Where I Want to Be

I'm from the Faulkner Hospital, trying to put weight as a four-pound baby. I'm from Mrs. Bradley who had two babies, one chubby, blue-eyed blonde, the other, known as the dark one.

I'm from Rita the housekeeper, who made blueberry pie, and Mom, the teacher, the reader of books which had the names like Lily and Rose in all print, no pictures book, and I vow to name my children Rose and Lily.

I'm from Dad, who said "five more minutes, girls" so we could for sure go to bed at seven while the neighborhood kids played out on Wren and Oriole streets, when it was light out and we were in our nightgowns.

But we had each other, Liz and I and Meb. We had Meb, who was from freckles and fair skin and magic and long chestnut hair, who won the Margaret O'Brien Look Alike Contest, while I was digging in the back yard with Mom's good silver, looking for China and talking to the fairies who would give me a dime under my pillow if I told them of a recent lost tooth.

And I'm from sister to John, who at five told us we could all put wet bread and towels outside of Cousin John Drummy's room, who was a teenager and our cousin, and we could bang on his door and for sure he'd come out and squish through this stuff in bare feet. What John my brother didn't tell was that Cousin John would grab me around the throat to throttle me, and what I didn't tell my aunt Esther, and my mom and dad, for that matter, that it wasn't that bad. Because you see I was too busy milking a newly acquired whine. I said instead, "Cousin John squeezed the breath out of me," and boy did he get in trouble.

And I'm from three years old when we had to live with Cousin John and Aunt Esther in their big old house, and there were bats down in the basement, and Rita had a sore bottom and begged, "Please stop crying," and I did because she asked me too.

But then I'm basically from Wren street, where I hugged Jesse the cat until his eyeballs squeezed out, and he trotted down the street to a Protestant household where he could eat filet mignon on Friday nights in a household composed of two elderly people who didn't clutch.

I'm from Mom, who when Mrs. Gravelese came in the door, and I had just settled on the floor in a rage of a tantrum, threw water on me, and I slunk away like a Disney skunk, ashamed and never threw a tantrum again.

I'm also from Mom closing the curtains because of a tobacco shortage during World War II, so she could smoke Dad's pipe, behind those blackout curtains, the same kind we had upstairs when we went to the bathroom and peed in the dark. I'm from jumping on cans for the war effort and turning in lard at the five-and-dime store. Did we actually turn in lard?

And later, I'm from the beginnings of Obsession, like collecting paper clips because they were the best hopscotch throwers in the world.

But actually, I'm from reading centuries of pain in Mom's eyes and resolving to never do anything wrong because she'd just look at me and I'd feel awful. Her looking at me was different from being chased all around the house by Rita, who pinned me down and spanked me with a hairbrush and I kicked her black and blue and then cried because I had hurt her and I apologized.

How could I forget I'm from St. Theresa's pointy-roofed Catholic Church, where Monsignor Donahue's forty-five-minute talks dealt with the danger of Communists lurking in the brand new spanking stucco building called the YMCA! I'm also from throwing up my First Communion and being afraid of Father Redding until he lead the girls' basketball practice sessions, and I became a forward and entered heaven because you could jump to the stars in basketball.

And I was free then...until we moved to Fernwood Road and we lost Uncle Bill Johnson, the man who was always there, who wrote letters and poems about dogs made of bones and meat, with corners at the end wrapped in hair. Uncle Bill Johnson, who gave Mom an oriental rug and said witty things and drew cartoons and always held me.

I'm from Mom staggering down the stairs to play Chopin as loudly as she could because they had electrocuted the Rosenbergs. I felt bad then, wondering if the lights around the United States would dim, as I sat on the couch with Ernie Don-a-something-or-other, trying to avoid his clutches because there was paper in my bra and I wouldn't grow until Hormone Replacement Therapy at 50, but that's another story and belongs under What I Became, but wait, let me remember some more.

I am from fudge and red mittens and West Roxbury Library books and endless sledding up and down the whole of Wren Street, from it's highest point near the Water Tower, where one summer it was reputed a man swung naked in the woods, so we called him Tarzan, but he was probably one of the guys who came back from World War II and just couldn't take it anymore, and what did we know of therapy and post traumatic stress?

I'm also from wanting to be a nun and naming myself Poor Clare after an autodidactic run through the West Roxbury Library's Books of saints to read of Poor Clare, who hung out with Francis, Francis of Assisi, that is, who beat his brother body bloody, and I would wonder about Self-Abnegation and being Poor in later years. Later, at that same West Roxbury

Library, I could rebelliously check out and return books by hiding them under an old trench coat, forgoing the required checkout at a counter. Maybe that's why I adopted St. Jude as the Patron of Lost Causes, because St. Jude would understand me.

And Today, in the What I Am Today, I have a St. Jude plastic aortic valve, and I think this free writing with this topic is great, and Eckhart Tolle might say that I am in the now. I will thank my friend Annie, who used this Who I Am exercise in her classes.

Energy Displaced — Breaking Coverage

Jumping into the secretarial pool, she broke the peace with displaced energy. You've come a long way, baby, but your place now is a place to push out words through the fabric of space. Words like "scream" and "tears" show up like salt drops on her lips as she witnesses the hour's sludge through the day.

"Now is the time for all good..." whatevers. Now is the time to rinse your soul with gray water and recite in penitent position, "Bless me Father, for I have used Whiteout on my toes ten times, whilst my ass has resented its ergonomic chair, and my neck has screamed about its meek position twice."

Perhaps the dispenser of penance would suggest, "Think of a few good men while the quick red fox jumps over the lazy dog," and, indeed, now is the time for all good men to come to the aid of a lost broken whatever.

So she tips up on her toes — an imagined aging Anna Pavlova, a virtual Isadora Duncan — and pirouettes her thickened way towards a glossy brown document box. She dumps her "job" on the stack, wondering all the while what it's like to be finished, outgoing, and not "coming a long way."

Back in her cubicle, the tweedy gray wool one, color wheel to her soul, she breaks her energy — bar, I mean — her energy bar with peanut butter and chocolate, displacing, for a moment, the wonders of living on a flat earth.

Kingdom By the Sea, a Modern Tale

It was many and many a year ago
when I worked for law firms weary, and
one night in the midst of document blight,
I longed for an end to my midnight dreary.
But nowhere then, or now, was there
an answer to my plight,
for I had, metaphorically speaking,
shot an arrow in the night.

It was Sweet Don Juan of Esquire Fame
who rendered me breathless and insane.
"Leave all for love," this lothario crooned
in my ear as each night as he held me
against the photocopy machine near,
until at last desperate I contacted
a dwarf reputed to be a seer.

"Blessings on thee little man. Whither and hither
hath my lothario ran?"
"I celebrate myself and sing myself,"
said the little man, "and why on earth
would you use incorrect verse?
No wonder he left you like
the gusty North Wind! I've seen this
loosening drift—it's breath—before."

"Dear maiden, build thyself stately
mansions in your heart, but never, ever,
ever listen to the man who orates and farts.
This Don Juan, so sweet in your purview
is known for how many maidens' hearts he slew.

Some day your true love will appear and be free,
 and you will live in a Kingdom by the Sea."
"Until now dear maiden, oh Stupid One,
leave thy job and be gone by One.
For no good comes to a legal lass
who falls for married men and cash.
Be strong, be brave, be true, be pure,
And do not come again as
I shall take you for an ass."

Split Decision (Spring 1983)
(for Tillie Olson)

She just couldn't go back.

It was the fear of returning, returning to the narrow, pale Dickensian chins, colorless competition with glazed blue eyes looking beyond and through her; the easing of their shapeless forms against cold leather chairs, pushing corporate words over, around and past her. The routine moments stretched and splattered, extending like a silent scream over the red and blue oriental rugs, over the Pollack and O'Keefe paintings on the wall, and over the bent, silent heads of the women: typing.

She had tried for years to be like the rest, tried to stuff the voice down that rose up, the "No" in her like the "No" of a Rosa Parks too tired to go to the back of the bus.

The "No" and the "Where am I going?" came out, like squabbling twins pushing their way to grab the front seat of the car, laughing, kicking, screaming towards the local drug store to see who got the Mars Bar first.

So now, the "No" had been handled and the "Where am I going?" was just sassing the hell out of her.

Where the "No" had been red and angry, volatile, insistent, the "Where am I going?" was tired, blue, fatigued, a dream gone poof, no white puffs to its sides, only wilted question marks about myths, and she could feel the underbelly of poverty, a shadow in the future. She was hesitating now, a question mark between things, wordless within worlds. She wondered about things: the career change, opinions of others and their queries, "Why can't you adjust?" and she bludgeoned herself for her restlessness.

But she couldn't go back, back to the inside of the gray—the gray that would convenience others, the gray that never questioned...the gray that cried inside against its seamless, eternal tediousness.

Dick Hart

I'm back to school after twenty years of being a legal secretary, still nursing chain indentations around my ankles. I'm big on metaphor, because after I looked the word up, I plunged into Literary Criticism classes (think Papal hierarchy). Now I'm real sick, and I can't seem to get better.

I am like a laundry chute. Feelings viral crawl and dump into my body, more so in February and March. I can barely drag around, not like a sad depression or clouds in head. But a patchy raggedness makes me feel weak. I have no resources, no energy stored, this after being able to run five miles on a track. In fact, I remember feeling strong until one day my energy left suddenly as if it were taking an elevator up and left me down on a bottom floor.

One day at UCI, I headed to the Humanities Building for a lit class. My hair was straight, my face was gray, and some friend said to me at lunch, "You look like a 1929 Communist intellectual." I rode my bike to the bike rack outside of Humanities, and I broke in a sweat when I pushed and pulled the bike into the rack.

The Student Health Clinic said, "Don't work, but still go to school." I still didn't have the energy to pull a sweater over my head. Still, lit class beckoned, and I sat next to my best friend, Jeff, another older student. He saved me the seat next to the wall in the back with him, in case I needed to just slump over. Our professor was to discuss one more author before finals—before the end of the quarter.

I felt more gray than usual, as the professor shoved titles of books down our throats, and, as promised, she introduced the last writer we would study.

I felt awful and sagged against the wall. I heard words through a fog, "Dick Hart, Dick Hart." I turned to Jeff, who was big and blonde, a real brain in literary criticism and said behind my notebook, my mouth slowing to elocute out "Who the @@**!!! is Dick Hart?" And then it dawned on me like a flickering twenty-watt light bulb. Descartes, Descartes, René Descartes, called the Father of Philosophy. Jeff and I broke out in a silent laughter, and later I crawled home like a weakened moth, but laughing all the way.

History of Language

In the beginning in the land of Iota, when the earth was new of sludge and drudge, when there was just the Word Pot and God, formally known as Old Ed ("OE" for short), and Sam Iam, his assistant, God was restless.

"Let us," He said, "Let us create some division, Sam Iam. Let us make two creatures. One shall be called 'man,' and we will name him 'Annee Moose,' and the other shall be known as 'woman,' and we shall call her 'Annee Mah,' and they shall compete."

"Tell them, oh Sam Iam, tell them they are to go forth with the Words from the Word Pot. Announce to them, 'Go forth from this Kingdom, this Kingdom of Iota.' Tell them OE issues them henceforth from this kingdom. Wish them 'God Speed' and 'Sally Forth,' and tell them, for God's sake, to leave the pot clean."

And so, it is written that Annee Moose got to the Pot first. For Annee Moose knew of the wisdom of Annee Mah and knew he needed a head start. And it appeared that strange words were at the top of this pot. So he scooped them out: piss, prick, pot, spoon, fork and oven. "I must go quickly," he thought, "to avoid Annee Mah." So off he clumped to the North to villages which would be called Germany and Norway and the rough, tough lands of men. And while he hunted and dressed in fur and roasted meat, he thought of his words. "Let me," he thought, "spray water into the air. And I shall call this water, 'Piss.'"

And Annee Mah, back in the Kingdom of Iota, came to the Word Pot. Words hiding deep in the bottom of the pot peeked out at her. They said, "I'm sorry, excuse me." Annee Mah's heart softened as she scooped the last of these sorry words to her bosom, and she ventured towards a kingdom soon to be called France.

But while Annee Moose used his oven and Annee Mah sorted her sorries, they were sad and knew of their aloneness. And they decided to come together. "Annee Mah," questioned Annee Moose, "My spirit is saddened, and I feel pricked by use of this oven. Could we not share and dwell together with our pots and spoons?" So it was that Annee Mah thought carefully and agreeably. "Further," spoke Annee Mah, "Why doth not we share our other words? Why doth not we betake of classical knowledge and share our body parts under the stars during the months and days of the week?" And Annee Moose and Annee Mah did just that very same thing, and Old Ed was pleased.

Writing Soup
(for Jack Grapes)

I am confused and bewildered in a house whose couches sprawl and sag and whose books give off musty odors as blonde, blue-eyed, white-toothed actresses sit together as on a bus of youth headed towards Pilates, thinking strength and prettiness will gift them the innate poem.

I sit across the room near three older women whose shadowed eyes reflect steel and pain, my eyes travel down to a patchy wood floor. My guts stick together like an old sandwich pressed too hard by the grill.

I feel as if I am in a stew or soup. Jack is the cook, but he isn't the cook. He is the Chef with a Capital C, with the "Write Like You Talk" recipe. Jack seems hot and fussy as if he's cooked soup for a long time. He stirs some long leggy carrots recently splayed from their leafy green tops. He pokes, bobbing "hi, I'm fresh from the farm" tomatoes into a plankton shape, and he flicks hot juice at the parsnips who turn into ciphers.

None of us move because we feel like bumpy vegetables.

I feel like a turnip, a rather purplish, solid turnip from New England—purplish on the top and yellow-white inside, but still a turnip—as I tilt away from the Cook. He takes a two-pronged fork and prods the parsnips and carrots again. Then he spears a medium-sized white potato, which grows soft, splits and sort of crumbles.

A zucchini leans into my purple side.

I feel contained and don't want to go near the Chef or the fork. I want to simmer and bob, when a chunky, juice-dripping piece of beef steams towards the center and waits for the Chef, who lifts up the beef with a slatted wooden spoon, admiring its contours and bursting juices.

He dips the beef back into the soup where all the vegetables get caught up by the juice's circular movement as the water around me gets browner and chunks of flattened red tomatoes float by and miss his hand which then spears and hauls me up dripping with the soup's flavors.

He puts me on a slatted spoon and turns me over with a slow, quizzical look. I am still a turnip, but I have become softer, more yellow-orange on the inside, ready to slough off some purple edges. I get put down again near the beef and tomatoes. I move closer to the carrots and the parsnips. We all mix with the broth.

Chiaroscuro

At writing class at UCLA extension, I stare at figures on a table. A clay face figure on this table disturbs me. Its three clear blue eyes gaze out. "Who are we behind our eyes?" I used to ask that of Jeff when we hung out in the UCI cafeteria, Jeff, putting salt and pepper shakers together, taking them apart. Jeff—my first brother of a friend, big blonde, intense blue eyes. Women circled around Jeff with silent crushes.

"Jeff," I'd say, after whining about Literary Criticism, telling him my knees locked midway towards genuflect position, asking him who was odiferous in Frank Lentricchia's class, "do you ever wonder who's behind the eyes or where your soul is?"

I wish Jeff were here for coffee so we could talk about chiaroscuro faces, like the one in front of me on the table with three eyes. I could tell him the eyes remind me of the three Bradley sisters when we were still sisters and lived on Wren Street.

Which eye made it? Where would Meb's eye be? What does the eye of a little girl who won a Margaret O'Brien look-alike contest show when it grows up and becomes alcoholic? And what about twins' eyes, the ones to the left and right of Meb on a bench after first communion or on the chiaroscuro figure in front of me in the writing class, on the flat table? I could use a sit-down-over-coffee-and-talk-to-Jeff time. Wall-eyed, maybe that's it. "We had to be walleyed and sit askew in a face that had more than one mouth and more than one point of view to survive it all." That's what Jeff would say. This mask on the table reminds me of the white snake skin and feathered mask Bill and I have which speaks of other dimensions and shadings and sorrows. It reminds Bill and me that life is never simple.

Tonight, I would like that mask on the table, the mask with earrings in its nose and ears, the mask which gives form to the unexplainable.

Functional Smunctional

"You're thirty-seven percent functional on the computer," Gary, the Personnel Manger, says as he hands me a long, slim aqua- and blue-colored brochure whose white letters say to me, "We're glad to have you on our team." The smaller print reads, "You have made a wise employment move."

It seems that, despite my red punk hairdo, which looks like it has been cut by my mother-in-law's old lawnmower, and my absence of computer use for more years than I want to recount, Gary is going out on a limb. Snelling Temporaries can be my new employer. Gary tells me, "You may call your Personnel Coordinator if you have any questions or if you are in doubt about anything."

Is there such a thing as a job where I wear my dream shoes which are red and green high top sneakers? A job where I could let my hair look like it had been cut by my mother-in-law's old lawn mower? Could I find a job where I could tell people how I really felt and we could we discuss books and writers? These questions tap danced within me at the Snelling office on a hot day in August.

Anything? How do I tell Gary, young, newly balding, black-haired Gary, "I practice the Zen of doubt?" Do Gary's earnest brown eyes, which twit toward my hair, understand underneath my skull lies trails of doubt, trails like those in an abandoned rabbit warren? Will Gary or my Personnel Coordinator comfort me about what's really on my mind? Does Gary know that besides living on a planet turning puce, I have personal concerns?

That night, I snivel in a telephone conversation with my husband who is in Buffalo, New York, on business. "I don't belong anywhere." He laughs and says, "That's why I married you. I like waifs." Just before he hangs up he says, "Don't rush into this, kid. It's been a while since you've worked. Give it time."

Earlier today I wanted to tell Gary, "Look Gary, I don't have the spit I used to. I'm at that age where women consider estrogen, and my face is beginning to resemble a yogurt raisinette."

I'd further tell him, "Maybe I'm not a Snelling gal after all. Gary, I can't seem to genuflect to attorneys any more." After that I'd work on leaping from thirty-seven percent computer literate to the ninetieth percentile. I had to go to work. Snelling would pay me more than two copies of a journal for writing an obscure article.

It's time to go back to the Big House on the plantation, I thought. "I wish you wouldn't refer to our law firm as 'the Big House,'" a Human Resource Director once said to me. What to do. Big House ways gonged at my psyche. Go into a building every day. Can't breathe. Sit. Type. Get up. Go out to lunch. Return. Sit. Type. Go home.

Maybe another employment agency will have something more creative.

The next day, I walk into Apple One at two o'clock, having sat in my car for an hour uttering, "I love it. I love it not," and then find myself inside Apple One's doors, my feet sinking into a deep plum carpet. My blouse and newly purchased scarf, which I can tie fifty-nine different ways, matches Apple One's carpet. It's a sign. Kathy, my Apple One employment counselor, is thrilled at her find. I type ninety-seven words a minute on their typewriters. She hands me a cardboard brochure which is long, white and purple and has a large red apple at the bottom right-hand corner with a bite out of it. My tummy begins to hurt.

I let Kathy and my brochure welcome me to the wonderful world of Apple One. They also promise me the excitement of being associated with some of the world's finest local and international companies. Where have I been? I can now meet more new people. Kathy's gray eyes turn to a light green as she tells me how important grooming is and some other facts. It seems the purple letters of my employment packet announce I should wear a dress. Kathy says in a half Valley Girl lilt, "We want our people to fit in and stand out only by their work performance."

She tests my word processing skills. There's a hitch. My typing speed has revealed paws of a chimp who can pick up sliced bananas from a hot black skillet in microseconds. My word processing knowledge, however, has gaps.

"Going back to a university was certainly commendable," Kathy says, smiling in a big tooth sort of way. "Nice you put down your six publications in the Iowa Women's magazine. We will need more from you to have as a base if you are to represent the Apple One World." Kathy's white teeth flash again, but this time her mouth appears dry and taut as if fingers are pulling the edges of her mouth sideways. "Never you mind," she says tossing her thick blonde hair back. "We're going to get you caught up. C'mon over and try these self-help manuals. They'll teach you all you need to know about word processing. We'll have you updated by five o'clock today and working by tomorrow." Kathy leads me to a small plum- and gray-carpeted cubicle.

Voices in my head hiss, "You're a cultural lag. Secretaries don't wear denim anymore, and your nails look like you play with cement." Secretaries now are young, slim and acrylic-nailed. Their hard and fast young nails whiz over computer keys like busy French poodle toes clicking across the kitchen floor towards a gourmet dinner.

I sit in my plum cubicle for two hours. I learn Word Perfect—again. I have copied, merged, deleted and blocked. Voices start filtering in. An employment counselor next to me interviews a girl with stringy brown hair. "What's your previous experience? What was your job description? What are you looking for?" I pause in a merge just to see the girl start chewing on a wisp of her hair. Words like "data entry, key punch, job too boring," whisper from her mouth and fall towards the plum carpet. Her employment counselor interrupts. "Look, you have to be enthusiastic. I work with one hundred applicants, and they have enthusiasm. I can't sell you without enthusiasm."

I return to document merge and try to block. I want to be a happy Apple One Employee, but the word "enthusiastic" claws my throat, and I stop blocking, deleting, adding, moving. Enthusiasm and acrylic nails are the new passwords. I have neither.

I slowly close Word Perfect's window and whisper, "Have a nice day," to my computer screen. I stand up, look around and give my broadest, cheeriest, teethiest goodbye to Kathy, hoping I don't look like an anxious ferret, and I head towards the door, the ocean and a bench where I can listen to the surf pound and decide about enthusiasm.

I think I'm going to write a story about secretaries and workers who want out. Maybe it will be a mystery, a thriller. My heroine will only be thirty-seven percent functional on anything, and I'll make her funeral a celebratory thing. How will she die? Who would come to such an event? A clerk type person dies. Who cares? But the women will come. The workers who know the ad, "You've Come a Long Way, Baby," and they'll think, Baby's dead, honey, and they'll come in droves. My Heroine, the secretarial candidate, will go to her death, transcending pain. She will burn for everyone, and I will get to her manner of death shortly, but meanwhile, how to dress her. Maybe a simple black skirt with a white silk blouse and a bow at the neck, tied under her chin, a sort of corporate cow bell.

She'll die carrying memories of a young girl who went to Boston Clerical School, who typed ninety-eight words a minute, who wore gloves to work as she clung to the straps of the subway car barreling its way into downtown Boston. She'll die for the secretaries who stayed in buildings and typed during bomb threats and who drank between 12:00 and 1:00 in order to handle between 1:00 and 5:00.

It won't be a simple funeral either—no traditional hop over to Forest Lawn. Nope—make a funeral bier from old manuscripts, legal secretarial books, resumes, employment applications. That will be the scene. Build the bier right outside the Santa Ana Courthouse, next to the jail and burn her at high noon, the lunch hour. Burn out the old. Burn in the new.

The women will arise at 12:00 and emerge from their buildings at 12:02, cross the street and surround the bier. Our Heroine will be their martyr, the one who knows and who went to her death, killing the idea of women happy pushing paper through machines. The women will wear small pins with circles around them and slashes against "a;sldkfj" and chant, "Ain't goin' to rush no more, no more; ain't goin' to rush no more," as the flames grow high and charred résumés fly outward into the air.

Gone will be the modulated voice who never said the eff word. Gone will be generational despair of words going through corporate deals, going through giant word mills, pushed by tired hands, voiceless mouths.

Someone will say, "Hush, look...," and above the bier, above the charred body and what once was a silk bow, an image will float. Our Heroine will have etherealized, but in a very colorful and savvy way, wearing jeans and a t-shirt. On her feet—"Oh, look at her feet!"—will dangle colored sneakers, red and green, up the ankle. A lawn mower will hang around our dead Heroine's neck like a locket. Her hair will be spiked, and she'll grin and wave. Then she'll fly away. But the women will cheer and turn to one another, link arms, and go off for an extended lunch.

Gary and Kathy of Snelling and Apple will be sad, but I will be enthusiastic.

Once More

It's the '90s, and I'm sick again. I've been sick since Christmas, since I worked in the law firm with blue silk winged chairs. I worry about being old in a culture that doesn't like old—and remember sick, too, not liking sick. But I don't come across that way.

I feel like a soul looking for a window through which to jump. I'm behind Epstein Barr bars and can't jump, and I've become a get-cured maven. I've eaten grains and I've taken a brown liquid called KM that caused my vet's dog not to drag his bottom across the floor. No more back problems for my vet's dog thanks to KM.

KM is a multi-marketing product that makes me so sick I slide under the coffee table. Muhtadia says, "Get off that stuff." Forget that Muhtadia takes the stuff, but her mother is allergic to it.

I once saw a psychic nutritionist who said, "The cure is Beiler soup, full of zucchinis"—and "No taste," I later add. I tried steam baths and saunas and maybe blasted my aortic valve into shrink and stiffen. I did therapy and antidepressants.

The biggest help was the fresh air of Seattle and Dan, my therapist. I also seemed better after I got my new heart valve, which ticked real loud, and I finally had physical energy. But now, I'm at the bottom of the barrel.

Dan would say, "It's depression."

Someone else would say, "Try some 12-Step Programs."

Someone else would suggest homeopathy, and what about herbs, acupuncture, Rolfing?

I've done it all, from woo-woo to straight. In Ottawa in '89, a Native American shaman worked on me. Drummed and hooted over my dendrites, and I felt better for a week or two. I've seen a Prussian nutritionist who charged $300 a month for vitamins. I spent an hour a week sorting out those vitamins. I've also seen the movie *Safe*, a sleeper of a film which deals with traditional medicine and new alternatives that meet up in an uptight vehicle of a gorgeous woman who can't breathe. I've decided to choose a grittier path. This gorgeous lady ends up in an igloo in the desert which is too West LA for me. But, oh me, oh my, now I'm struggling again. But, I'm still writing and going on a book tour. I'll just have to lie down a lot in between.

Elizabeth Farnsworth, Where Are You?
Jamestown, New York (1998)

I sent *Without a Net: a Sojourn in Russia*, my book regarding our life in Ukraine and Belarus and a visit to Siberia in 1990-1993, to Elizabeth Farnsworth of *The News Hour with Jim Lehrer*. I've seen Ms. Farnsworth interview literary figures. She's kind and intelligent. I believe Elizabeth has a thinking heart. She replied, penning her response on a small sheet of powder blue stationery that said, "Senior Correspondent."

Elizabeth Farnsworth said she's looked through the book, and she hopes to read it soon, and it's not time for a segment yet. I didn't tell her my husband and I live like graduate students, and unless I receive extra money, I will never be able to go back into Ukraine. I didn't tell her the Ukrainians and Russians become your soul's friend and that I honored their feelings and loyalty and felt my soul had to be brave enough to go back; to touch a face; laugh over tea; share a smile; give and receive hope.

Oh, I forgot to tell her I'm applying for the fellowship grant for $1,000 to go back into Belarus and maybe Ukraine, if the trains and borders don't close up. Why on earth would I go back to a country whose economic situation is like rubber ice and thaw—also known as economic collapse? Well, it's a call, because I am half wimp and half lioness, but I'll leave my wimp behind.

My friend Ralph, in Chico, California, said, "You'd go to Russia on $1,000?" Then he said, after listening to my pit bull grip on the idea of going back in April, "Well if you get $1,000, I'll match it." This all means that I can go back and reestablish relations and write a sequel to my book. I will witness daily events, which events may be much grimmer since 1993, when I flew home, tossing my cookies all the way. I'm not going because I like adventure and riding in grubby trains which reek of urine and waiting in the Kiev Railroad station at night. One Sunday night in Ukraine, as we staggered through that station with heavy duffel bags, a Ukrainian friend said, "Dante forgot to include this." I'm also not going so I can drink tea that bounces off my tummy and boil water and expect nothing to work.

I'm going because I want to give voice to the human condition. I want to give my sideways glances towards ordinary lives. I want to give a voice to people who wouldn't have a chance to say who they are, how they love, what they fear, what makes them laugh, what makes them cry. I can do this. As a writer, I could go to Seattle and write about the birds, flowers and the complexities of urban life. That would be safe, but I try to be a hollow reed reflecting the currents of our time.

This is my definition of a true writer. I know every step of my trip might be uncomfortable. I'll be wrapped in love and care, though. Some protective voice will order tickets in Russian for me. Others will hug and smile, and we will talk at our deepest level. I will be filled up and be brave (until I get home). Then, I'll write of these events and, once more, I will be forever changed because of writing of the human condition. It's like being in the shadow of Anna Ahkmatova. I have a need to give voice to those who can't speak.

So I hope people will read my new essays and say, "Elizabeth Farnsworth, where are you? Have you read this? Can we talk?"

Statement of Purpose (Applying for a Grant) — (Constance Saltonstall, Where Are You?)
Jamestown, New York (February 1999)

"Driven," comes to my mind. That's my statement of purpose. It's economically packed, to the point, and used well when life is engaged on the fly. I started writing in my forties when I returned to university life. At the time, I was a single mother, and I had a son who could have rolled an army tank over me without a blink of an eye. I had mono and Epstein Barr Virus, had to work part time, all the while gashing myself on points of literary criticism.

I was encouraged to write, and I haven't stopped (except for maybe six months here or there after brutal criticism). Now, I am married, am older: a teacher of writing; a racial justice advocate; and a substitute teacher in a town where minimum wage and three jobs are viewed as normal. Don't forget to add I may be wife to Bill, but I am daughter-in-law to Anna, who is eighty-six and could spit cannon balls out of her mouth at a moment's notice. My life is my material. I thrive on chaos. "Grist for the mill" is carved on my Fly's Saddle.

I need time off and a better computer. I would have filled out the requests for Artist Residencies, but I really can't afford the time without some income squeaking in. Bill is a wonderfully supportive husband who is now on early Social Security. Thus, we live like graduate students, but I take risks.

We went into Russia at a time when our income went poof and thoughts of future solidarity left the planet. Still I write. I write pain and humor, and I am a creative, nonfiction, hang-around-the-corner-at-coffee-shops type of person.

What would I do with the grant funding? I tell the Saltonstall grant people, "I'd write an essay about the Physics of Puggy and his ever humble and glorious ways. When he pees, he looks like Nureyev. Need I say more? I'd collaborate on a screen play about Vasili Vasilivitch, gulag survivor (from my book *Without A Net: A Sojourn in Russia*)."

Constance Saltonstall, where are you? "I'd write about life in Jamestown, New York. I'd talk about Walter, an older African-American whose tension of the opposites roars within him. Walter is a chief figure in our Downtown Race Dialogue group. I'd write about my next trip into Russia (this spring if funded) for a month and describe life in Ukraine and Belarus, where conditions have worsened, are grittier and hard to believe. I'd also write about the love of Russian friends encircling me."

"I'd write all this hunkered down with Puggy in a cold basement, next to my computer's dim light. This basement is part of my mother-in-law's house about which any Feng Shui expert would 'tsk, tsk.' Given time, I'd turn out spunky, heart-lightening prose, stories of pain, guts, and love. I'm a mix, because I write and dash about. I need time (oh, how I hope you consider this plea for a grant).

"Oh, and one more thing. I'd go down to Kaldi's Coffee Shop on Third Street, have a big slug of coffee, smile and say to Tony, Loretta, Laurie and the gang, 'I just got a grant. Did you ever hear of Constance Saltonstall?' Then, of course, I'd have to find out about this lady who has made things possible for those artists inch-worming their way through life." (Reader: I didn't get the grant, but I went back to Ukraine and Belarus for six weeks in September 1999.)

Getting a Lifestyle

- ☐ Go to Chautauqua for "Get a Lifestyle" class.
- ☐ Pray red car works. Ask God for car engine to work. Ignore muffler noises.
- ☐ Go to Sadie J's for last Cappuccino muffin, coffee with designer creams. Give up junk food by Friday.
- ☐ Visualize life, health, energy, balance. Finish coffee and muffin. Rush to class.
- ☐ Write suggested affirmations. Say them out loud and touch scar on chest which still hurts.
- ☐ Learn of goodness of greens. Learn body, mind and spirit not separate. Diet cola dehydrates. Scan memory bank for epochs of drinking vats of diet cola, troughing silos of sugar, rolling in mountains of white flour.
- ☐ Imagine your bones potato chip thin.
- ☐ Resolve to do affirmation, "I will no longer refer to my bones as potato chips, or my hips as turtle shells."
- ☐ Have coffee after class.
- ☐ Order hummus at Sadie J's. Eat potato chips with hummus. Go to writing workshop. Whine about birds and Chautauqua's elite.
- ☐ Go to race dialogue meeting at Hurlbut. Tell stories and hang out in Bestor Plaza over dinner of huge chocolate chip ice cream cone.
- ☐ Drive home.
- ☐ Notice audible noises from back of red car. Take nap. Listen to mother-in-law Anna talk about bad tummy.
- ☐ Watch Anna tune into TV program with Mother Angelica. Go down to basement. Write homework.
- ☐ Make a note, "Mother Angelica looks pasty—too much roast beef"?
- ☐ Drive to Chautauqua.

- ☐ Wonder about funny noises at back of red car. Get only coffee at Sadie J's. Notice shortness of breath. Slug down coffee.
- ☐ Go to health class. Get hug coupon. Resolve to do serious hug exchanges with Pug Dog at home. Learn of green drinks. Learn of chicken hell.
- ☐ Have salad and regular coke at Sadie J's.
- ☐ Go to writing group.
- ☐ Listen to heavenly essay on raspberries.
- ☐ Go home.
- ☐ Plan to work out. Take nap instead.
- ☐ Wake up.
- ☐ Make peanut butter and jelly sandwich, roll it up into fist, and pour big glass of milk.
- ☐ Listen to Anna talk about her tummy.
- ☐ Go to basement and wash Pug.
- ☐ Look at basement's green walls. Write essay about mother.
- ☐ Eat Anna's chocolate chip cookies (ten if you must know) and read.
- ☐ Collapse into bed.
- ☐ Drive to Chautauqua in the a.m.
- ☐ Ignore loud rattle from back of red car.
- ☐ Learn of green drinks and living food.
- ☐ Integrate knowledge. Think diet cola and potato chip world near impending doom.
- ☐ Meet Bill. Eat salad.
- ☐ Buy fortune cookie, "Prepare for impending life decisions." Order regular Pepsi. Resolve to give up cola.
- ☐ Talk to friend's depressed daughter.
- ☐ Go to writing workshop.
- ☐ Laugh and grunt inappropriately at writing workshop filled with Wellesley graduates of yesteryear.
- ☐ Go to auto mechanic.
- ☐ Auto mechanic laughs at car's innards, "They look like a 1945 junk yard."
- ☐ Leave car.
- ☐ Go home.
- ☐ Plan to work out.

- ☐ Take nap instead.
- ☐ Spread peanut butter and jelly into some bread, grip in hand, and take out door.
- ☐ Go to Race Dialogue Meeting in evening.
- ☐ Have coffee with dietician friend and eat nonfat yogurt with nonfat fudge Sundae.
- ☐ Talk about chickens, dairy, greens, and life in Guyana, and paper making.
- ☐ Go home. Say long prayers. Fall into bed.
- ☐ Take 74 VW bus to Chautauqua.
- ☐ Go to health class.
- ☐ Learn of generational disintegration. Does that mean cars too? Learn your body acidic enough to hiss black smoke. Learn about alkaline.
- ☐ Resolve to give up ice cream and diet cola tomorrow. See friends.
- ☐ Plan to work out.
- ☐ Get interviewed on radio. Talk about life in Russia.
- ☐ Head for workout.
- ☐ Go home instead.
- ☐ Visualize health food stores and cooking tofu.
- ☐ Make peanut butter and jelly sandwich.
- ☐ Take to basement and read "Girl." Write.
- ☐ Talk to neighbor across street. Note her brother sells used cars.
- ☐ Head for bed. Collapse between Bill and Pug.
- ☐ Get up early and take VW Bus to Chautauqua.
- ☐ Rush in for coffee. Go to interview with Jim Roselli on local radio program from WJTN.
- ☐ His first question: "What exactly did you mean by 'old white boys in Jamestown?'"
- ☐ Late for health class.
- ☐ Go to writing workshop.
- ☐ Go to Hurlbut for chairs for open mike readings on Packard Manor Porch.
- ☐ Put out lemonade, cookies, and chairs. Listen to lady speak of Chautauqua as a religious experience. Listen to lady speak of "moneyed people" helping out.

- ☐ Listen to mahogany-skinned young woman speak of blood running down a wrist. Intake breath and feel purity and passion of a first reader.
- ☐ Listen to juggler talk of limericks, tell stories of tricks.
- ☐ Unload chairs at Hurlbut.
- ☐ Go home.
- ☐ Make peanut butter and jelly sandwich.
- ☐ Open birthday cards from friends and eat two fudgesicles. Wonder if son will call.
- ☐ Eat small Tootsie Rolls. Resolve to finish them up.
- ☐ Fall into bed. Telephone rings. Have riotous conversation with Margaret about psychotic principals with face lifts.
- ☐ Listen to phone ring before midnight.
- ☐ Hear son's voice. Notice cells inside of body perk up. Fall back into bed. Plan to give up diet cola Monday.
- ☐ Note: Write piece on lifestyle.

Peking Noodle Company Saves the Day (January 1997)

My 93-year-old, last-of-the-Imperialists aunt drives us to Chinese food Monday night. I want to hang my throat on a hook, but let Bill sit in front with her and cringe at the highway. This aunt, whom I love, files you in two categories: rich or famous. To hear her tell it, "A nephew makes billions in copy work, while a granddaughter's husband is a well-known actor." My aunt often tells me her first husband was the brightest man in the Navy, and her second husband, who was a producer, was good with money, and of her almost-to-be-third husband who was a general, who at 95 proposed, but died two weeks before the wedding, which became a funeral.

Bill and I have a '74 Volkswagen bus and a monthly income multidimensional marketing men sneer at. I think we are not in her categories. You see, when I married Bill, he made a lot of money. Somehow my aunt makes him into Italian royalty, despite the fact his mother is like a small sturdy tree trunk and doesn't take nothin' from nobody and only graduated from junior high.

My aunt is the prettiest old lady in the United States. She has luminous white hair and a patrician air, and she dresses as if she's going to a college reunion. "Never know," she says, "I might meet someone." At the restaurant, we choose Chicken Something-or-Other and Broccoli Beef and Sweet-and-Sour Pork. Bill and I talk loudly so she can hear us. She won't wear a hearing aid, and she told us—and the rest of the restaurant for that matter—how good it is to be a Republican because "they're not corrupt."

"You're sort of retired now," she says to Bill. "Yeah," he says, and to her "Do you make any money?", he says, "No. Did, but not right now." She laughs an "Oh, dear," soft-throated money laugh, and I want to hang my head between my knees and cry. I remember a past visit with my father and stepmother, who told of a grandchild of ten who was a very good writer. My stepmother turned towards me, "Why do you write?", as she spoke of her sons—my stepbrothers—one, a professor, the other an ambassadorial post, with wives at Harvard and Radcliffe.

But back in Leisure World, at the local Chinese Restaurant, I put on a smile when my aunt, the only one at our table who uses chopsticks, says, "Honey, your hair needs thinning," and, "You've got to make money with your book," while I wonder, how on 1,000 copies, self-published? Just then our fortune cookies arrive. She hands a cookie to each of us.

The last time I had a fortune cookie of note was with my writer friend, Stephany. I had said, "Steph, I don't know where I'm going," and opened up my cookie which was blank. But Bill's fortune cookie said to him this Monday night, in the big plain, maroon Naugahyde booths, where we sit across from my aunt, "You are a bundle of energy, always on the go," and I know this to be true, almost psychic, to be exact. Then I open my cookie, and the Peking Noodle Company says, in blocked, red Times New Roman letters, "Your talents will capture you the highest status and prestige." I tell you, though, that night, over the plain white rice and Sweet-and-Sour Pork and Broccoli Beef, I felt less like a cork bobbing on the ocean of despair.

The Street at 8 a.m.

It's loaded with people,
not so loaded
that I can't kitty corner to the
cross walk to Peet's
to meet someone who
has caught her edges on a thorn
and me too. I have the same type
of thorn, except this is about really
her, me, us, and I started it
by writing a letter regarding
what I called group behavior.
Maybe it had to be said,
but what I've learned is I
should have gone to her first.

Yeah baby, just because you felt the thorn
didn't mean you had to assign a place
for her. Maybe I don't mean that. What I
mean is I wouldn't hurt her for the world,
and I like her, except the edges of my personality
and her personality, hit and clashed. Maybe
because I'm often with Mr. Bill which some equate
to the B&E Show. Our styles are different.

So she thought we'd just meet for milk with vanilla
for me, and black coffee for her, and we'd talk.
She might have thought we wouldn't talk about
my being afraid to go up to her, and my feeling walls.
She wouldn't know what I meant.
It boils down to her being a very neat lady

who can be as strong as a fresh wind coming
down the freeway. I don't want to assess her, and
she was quick to say, ""I'm not ready to be
assessed.

We talked about other things; basically,
the universal heart of Moms who have grid marks
on their souls. I tell you, I felt a lot better, and
I should have done this two years ago, but I didn't,
and that's the facts, Jack. But it's not facts, it's about
 perceptions, but facts goes better with Jack.

Otherwise we are like American travelers who
trot into communities across that thing they
call the Atlantic Ocean, which is big and
looks like blue Jello that fell out of the frig and
don't you know, crosses more than geographic
boundaries, but is full of cultural expectations
and, "This is the way we do it here."

Never make the mistake of saying
"In the U.S. we do it this way;" because
what you really should do is say, "Hi; glad to be here.
I'll be quiet and sit back, but quiet and sitting back
aren't Bill's or my style, so we have to be careful and
not come on like the Bobbsey Twins
as if everyone has read us and knows who we are.

No one should feel less, and I've spent a lot of my
early years feeling less. I don't want to contribute
to that state of being. So here at Peets, over
the steamed milk with vanilla which goes
to the bottom of my tummy and makes me
feel alright with life, our humanness revealed,
we take out the thorns together.

Late Shift at the Poem Factory
(for Jeff Utter, our Interfaith Angel, on the occasion of his 60th birthday)

I. (ASSIGNMENT)

Describe man in five words?
Describe man — seven syllables?
I cheated, and second line was eight
Okay, at 10:46 p.m. get the hang of it.

Write a poem about Jeff
Jeff The Utter that is!
Try for a crooked haiku
The math-impaired haiku

II. (WRITING THE POEM)

Multisyllables; multiman; multidimensions
Chaplain fits better than minister.
Is minister contained in community?
Rather, Chaplain heart contains community within?

If I were a betting person,
I'd bet on a lot of things.
One thing for sure,
I'd bet on the pure-heart

Of the Chaplain/Minister with the Bird of White.
I'd bet he's surfed the waves of invisible Prayer
Traveled in and out of the Kingdom of Love
Love for his Lord that is ... love shown ...

In a Veteran's eyes of blunted pain,
Mankind's disjointed plight.
Maybe he's one of those arrows that goes
Right to the Center—the center of things

Like we are one, and let's enter into Faith.
Let's, as a matter of fact, Interfaith;
Make it a verb, yeah,
Let's do interaction action!

Then there's the multifaceted man
Who is ten when he says,
"Would you like to see my Bird"? and
Smiles a delicious, private, still-hovering-on-ten smile

While Chappie, the dove, takes flight
across the room!
Precursor to our purpose
Being in a heads-up room and place

'Tis a time for this man of Faith,
When the souls of all of us
Gather for flight; yeah
an action type of thing

III. (SUPERVISOR'S SUGGESTIONS)

Too grand to fit the humble haiku
Next time, writer, try a sonnet!

You Carry the Heavy Stuff

Do you see the way the new leaves curl and crisp? Those dark trees, with rough bark of gray and black, hold memories. There's DNA remembered here in Western New York. Anna, my mother-in-law, is gone, an untenanted room now and remembered thoughts of an indomitable little figure.

The trees seem slender, tight after a cold winter, but now in March, winter ebbs.

A pug dog, a very fat, spoiled pug dog, walked in his harness in Allen Park. Oh, the DNA of Pugs. I want to draw a dot-to-dot picture, a line drawing of the Physics of Our Pug! I want to show when he died and what cell went to what bush, what tree, or caught on someone's shoe in Allen Park.

Bill and I walked this path a lot. Allen Park was an oasis away from Anna's small bungalow house, white frame, black shutters, tidy, fearful, a home with light switch plaques of the Virgin Mary and Child, pink and white crocheted Afghans over a maple frame bed, a Catholic Girl's room at five. Anna in the kitchen, cooking the sauce, the sausage, and her cookies gave Puggy a new handle. Puggy became "Lardo," and Anna's kitchen helper. Along with the "sauce" and her famous fried-in-Crisco veal cutlets with canned peas on top and mashed potatoes swimming in butter, Anna cooked her famous cookies every week. Some cookies were vanilla S-shaped with pink frosting on top.

My drug of choice called to me in the form of Anna's chocolate chip cookies. They were small, warm, friendly, and promised me the moon and an eternity of feeling safe. I'd eat ten at a sitting. I'd then stagger back through our low-ceiling narrow hallway, past a room which housed a surplus of Infant of Prague statues, past and away from Sister Angelica's voice on the TV, made purposely loud to make Bill and me come back, come back to the Mother Church.

Was it four years we spent there? I moved all my books to the basement, leaving Anna's living room with her one book. Anna said, "All those books! Why?" Anna, whose life was book-ended by tradition of what to cook and what to eat. Anna was book-ended by rites of spring cleaning, fall cleaning, wash, iron, cook sauce, and make pizza. Anna, all four feet of her, closed all the drapes in the house at five o'clock on the dot, and she ran a tight little house.

When I met Anna, she had just come from the funeral home where Milo, her husband of many years, lay. Anna came down the hallway towards a back bedroom, and I emerged to meet her for the first time. Bill and I were recently married. She flung her arms around me, and as I enfolded her, I felt as if I were embracing a very small, but talking, tree trunk. "Milo, Milo, Milo," she said to my rib cage, "This is your daughter-in-law." "Milo, Milo, Milo," Aunt Sarah and a few relatives were within hearing distance nearby. Anna and I stood and hugged for what seemed a very long time.

After the funeral, after the funeral breakfast in the long, low-slung basement room of St. James Roman Catholic Church, after relatives sitting, eating, talking on her brown and orange furniture, after a lot of sauce covering spaghetti like a sacred veil, we packed to go home. I stood by the car, putting our bags in the trunk. She moved in right next to me. Bill was in the house. I heard a low voice say, "You—you carry the heavy stuff for him." I think, "Did she really say that"?

Miss Halloran

Before summer begins on a hot, flat-clouds, blue-sky June day, Jannie, Liz and I walk away from Randall G. Morris Elementary School. We take a quick turn onto Oriole Street, away from Wren Street, and take the long stretch down Bellevue Street; across Centre, past the West Roxbury Library, left and into the Robert G. Shaw Junior High School. We are here to see our seventh-grade teacher, Miss Halloran. She likes to meet her next year's students in June.

Girls with pink lipstick, shocking pink lipstick, clump together, while Jannie, Liz and I find seats fairly near the front of the room. This room is large, cavernous compared to our small room of elementary school.

I see a small figure at the front of the room. She's tidy, like a sparrow, and she has brown and gray hair, full, blowsy, not contained. Her hair looks like a bird's nest, and she wears glasses that fall onto the tip of a small nose. Then I scan the room, avoiding the girls with pink lipstick, until my eyes fall upon a large poster on the wall. It's a cartoon strip in black and white. The teacher likes cartoons?

The first panel shows an ape man, with big hairy arms and a club, as he tends a fire. I imagine he grunts and is greasy and smelly. The second panel shows warfare with soldiers lined up in serried rank, like book ends, opposite one another. They fire long-stemmed rifles at each other, and clouds of smoke appear in the upper right hand corner of the drawing. The third panel shows army tanks and helmets that look like pineapples on top of men's heads, and bigger clouds of smoke. The fourth, next to last panel, shows a huge cloud in the sky which looks mushroom-shaped. Near this giant mushroom are quickly drawn lines of thunder bolts, and an explosion. Finally, the last panel shows the same hairy, greasy, grunting, ape man by the fire.

My world view is changed forever.

Before the Golden Age

Elizabeth Vargas bids goodbye from the news. Wait! How is Peter Jennings? Now I know of his kind heart, his last days, his frailty—but what of his regrets about those last cigarettes?

Nine/Eleven—my fingers probe memory's silt, and Braille the reality of those days, and touch upon Terror's dullard cousin, Disbelief. Our earth stood still on Nine/Eleven. Together, in cylindrical need, we lurched towards one another in a oneness prayer of no words, no syllables, no sounds.

We were united until the politicians of cacophonous tilt, like crows from New Jersey, fat cigars hanging from their mouths, carped, scavenged and hawked their way up ladders of avarice and greed, all the while cavorting along the back halls of the politically elite and power's salacious divide. Language used for dark, reptilian thoughts separated the enemy, the other. Did I say crows? I meant boys, boys at play, like gargoyles in a game, like crocodiles shopping for dental twine.

Road Kill

Visualize the earth from that first soul-gasping view of outer space. See its perfect roundness—large, solid, resplendent in this first virginal glimpse. A planet before it goes to dancing school, adolescent, self-conscious, thinking only it exists. Imagine the earth's surprise; did I say the Earth's surprise? Imagine you, the observer's surprise, as your eyes widen, your corrugated views fall away like old siding. We are not the only ones.

Visualize, if you will, a full moon, illuminating this gut-soothing view of the planet. Wait. Blocks appear to circumambulate the earth's rim. Like gargantuan sow bugs in deliberate plod, these blocks move. Your eyes narrow as these steel carriers, like expanded versions of high school lockers, move in a relentless grind, gouging the planet's surface. They grunt and suck as you stand riveted.

Visualize these silhouettes which you now recognize as Humvees. Another light appears, like a distant point, the size of an eraser on a pencil, building in intensity. This light folds over the Humvees, casts a splash of light on to the Earth's inky blue covering. Then the light hovers, wiggles, and finally stills. A hot revulsion fills you as the light reveals a place, a city twisted, rotted, bombed-out, dusty—carcasses on the street, children crying without limbs, homes, or parents. Baghdad. The light reveals Baghdad.

You awaken.

Children of the Stolen Ones
(for Gloria Haithman—December 2, 2004)

"Greens" makes me think of Ola Mae's Greens, down in my belly, in Olean, New York, as crowds of us burst into Ola Mae's Restaurant on a regular basis to shoot the breeze, eat her famous Greens, and just to feel all's well with the world. Here in Pasadena, California, the subject of greens and chitlins came up. I thought of Ola Mae, the camaraderie, her corn bread too, and just feeling part of the woodwork welcomed by her open heart and Best-Greens-Cook-In-The-World self.

In Pasadena, on a Wednesday night, Gloria talked about the same thing, but went a step further. She spoke of soul food on another level, the spiritual teachings of love, hope, and faith. She spoke to our insides where there are no colors. Gloria said, "We were not colored when we were born. Yeah, I thought, we came in that way, and no one crayoned some in, or bleached others out.

What if, instead of calling the dark ones, the Negroes, the People of Color, names given by history book scribes, say, "Black or African-Americans?" Then a phrase measured out, by Gloria, entered our gathering, all the while she was telling of a story of friends who called themselves The Sisters. These Sisters went to South Africa, honoring their roots, and seeking answers to their identities. On the trip they were constantly greeted by groups of women who would sing to them. One day they met some African women who had the "Who are You? Where are you from?" look in their eyes, all the while staring at The Sisters.

One of the South African women said, "They are Children of the Stolen Ones." Back in Pasadena, sitting on the orange velvet couch, those small noble words, "The Stolen Ones," bombarded my heart as I felt my soul sink into a place of utter knowingness, of a reverence and majesty revealed.

As a white lady, an older one, who learned of our essential oneness some forty years before and humbly stayed on the thorny and pitted path of discovery and unity, I sat there stunned. I repeated the phrase over and over to myself. "Children... Children of the... Children of the Stolen Ones...."

Yes, and for me it was a rightful and merciful appellation.

Finally, dignity and solace packed into five words. Measure it out on the tongue, slowly: "The Stolen Ones... Children of the Stolen Ones." Feel your heart melt as if a great and timeless grief has finally been acknowledged.

My heart bowed a humble bow to the true nature of an incredible people, their majestic endurance, their ancestors. I'm no artist and don't know my colors, and I live in a world that thinks it knows its colors, and colors inside the lines, not outside—the "lines" being the operative word.

Well, I'd say in this year of 2004, "Maybe we should hear The Sisters, our sisters', call from South Africa," and use lines to wrap around: Majesty, Dimension, Endurance, Courage. Name every quality our sisters and brothers of African heritage carry with fortitude, and you come up with, in my book, "The Chosen Ones." And, what if God and his Messengers and Prophets saw that these Chosen Ones endured trials similar to the Minor Prophets? And what if Bahá'u'lláh knew His love for His Chosen Ones, knew they suffered the banishment, the chains, the whippings, as He, in the Path of God?

So here's the final what if—what if this planet really was a testing ground to see who could show courage under fire, love of God, love of people despite that the Stolen Ones and their kin were also robbed? But wait, here's another view. I think the Children of the Stolen Ones are the Morning Glories of our age! Their children; their children's children. It's the story Morning Glory.

Let's proclaim, let's shout, and let us bow in reverence to our ancestors, ransomed so we might reframe our hearts and join each other in history's future where lines are a thing of the past and colors are loved-filled stripes of every hue.

Skin Color

At the Black History Parade, put on by the Jackie Robinson Center, one cold, but sun-emerging day, paralytic agony stops my nouns, verbs and adverbs describing skin color or lack thereof. Pain fills my heart as my eyes Braille the sadness of a man's face, deep rivets line his cheeks, highlighting generational discounts and the pitter patter of white voices.

Numbness clots my throat at this morning's Parade, while those in other parts of the city, those from White gulags, tuff lawns, buff cars, and spread glossy interracial magazines, photo ops on tables, never viewed by the living.

Brown vs. Board, wasn't that in Topeka?

In Idaho, Bill and I share a table with a Nigerian psychiatrist. It's lunch time, and Bill asks a question which floats over our salads:

"Do you have to emphasize your African heritage"?

An acknowledged "Yes."

A rueful, half-stated reply, "My children will not have that advantage."

On the broad palettes of television's life experts on society, are noticeable by their absence of color. Hey, what about *The News Hour with Gwen Ifill*? Yeah, and Colin Powell, and... Yeah? Hey guys, take the tour of Any City, USA, where two separate neighborhoods exist—bookends of ideological contrast. One is spacious, forgiving, and tolerant, with wide streets, large houses and gracious plants, suggesting it's easy to feel benevolent. The other part contains narrow streets, boards on windows, hunger at night, restless poverty, and shootings. Skin color privilege cuts its wide swath.

I can say no more.

Seeing *Syriana*

Writing poetry, which speaks of white skin-color privilege, of seeing underwear ads, with thirty-year olds, trim in their Hanes, pornographic in their Victoria's Secret, won't translate into a haiku. How do you haiku frustration, absence, a feeling of Gargoyles 24, Unicorns 0? It was the film that did it. *Syriana*, a word or words manufactured like Xerox, or Aluminium, Ltd., or Pepsi. Except Syriana means a carved out territory, made up of whatever lands are useful to the dominant powers in need of oil.

Long story short, the film *Syriana* is brave and profound, staggering in its mirrors of global duplicity. Somehow the bad guys seem in charge and urgency screams, "Open your eyes." Do you recall memory's soft song, "Do you know where you're going to? Do you know, do you know?" This song ribbons my brain, and my cilia pushes sounds and concepts in a direct route to my heart.

I write of daily moments. I write of the turn of a wrist, hairs caught in a watch band, a tired dark hand clinging to a subway strap—two years of dirt on the homeless lady at California and Lake. I write of overheard conversation at Peet's while sitting at round, glossy wooden tables, our laughter vaulting towards Peet's high ceiling. I write of moments—shattered and reassembled.

Peace, that illusive dancing creature, is tossed about like an old crouton, nicely mentioned on street corners. Peace is politically correct on placards and bumper stickers. It's like a white handkerchief fluttering in one's hand, noiseless, an image and moment of no consequence. Attaining peace seems like the sound of blossoms falling on rippled water. Don Marquis, who wrote *Archy and Mehitabel*, said writing verse is "like throwing rose petals down the Grand Canyon." Well then, what is working for justice, while the guys in back halls cavort along vortexes of greed for today and tomorrow's oil? Danger: implosion ahead. Are we standing on the edge of the Decline and Fall of the Roman Empire, Scene II, in the years 2000 and on? Y2K had nothing on this.

And yet, a voice—make that voices—of those who know of the coming of the promise of a divine justice, the spawning of ordinary peoples coming together for global oneness and unity, begins to be heard. A curved, small ray of moonlight in the darkened sky with no sounds of blossoms falling is a symbol of man's hope and goodness, pointing towards the future—suggesting solutions. Like a sliver of the moon, time will reveal the fullness of moons, our shift away from the shaking frame of a beleaguered mankind.

It's an old jail, and we have to leave. A new race of man will struggle towards its destined spiritual maturity, a webbing of clusters of ordinary people, helping one another, preferring others instead of a self, all in stark relief against night's darkness of greed and hatred. The blossoms seem noiseless but startling white as they fall into the future.

On the Page

"Be on the page," she cries. What color is it? Blue, I hope, the deadness of old eyes. Nothing left to think.

"In the Book is a better place," he sighs. Green is a God color Muhammad and His Turban, The Báb, and so it goes.

Brown dust of civilization, horse hoofs thunder over past lives. Generations silenced by lives of spin. On TV voices blandly erase America's soul.

Cutting edge isn't the edge of a cucumber, or pickle, or nails buffed in Beverly Hills' salons. Surface street ads scream along with humanity. Someone in Afghanistan is homeless, and yet the page is blank.

When do we fill our pages, with sun warming our backs, white men telling the truth? No more technology rape. Why not be orgasmic? Spiritually orgasmic? Ritualism is death to the psyche.

TV kills; politicians kill; spin circles the drain. Art imitates life, but life destroys art, and so here we are in the Kingdom of Names.

It's Still the Same Old Story

It seems the same. Archetypes bump into one another, and a scene is repeated. Visualize yourself at a circus. See the strong man hit the bell: Praetorian Guard 1, Roman citizen 0.

Did they have education problems at the beginning of the decline and fall of the Roman Empire? Was it only lead in their wine goblets which did the Empire in, or did a whole coarsening society shudder its way beyond the pale? Meanwhile, back at the Games, a lion chomps on an extra meaty bone as the crowds, ever tense in the present moment, cheer.

We have arrived where we began some dusty centuries ago. Does the ordinary citizen want to slit his or her throat? Does anyone want to scream, gash eyeballs and wonder why we haven't been nuked? Back in the time of the Caesars, if I remember the "I Claudius" series correctly, only the seemingly stupid survived. Claudius with his Praetorian Guard made it. The rest of his relatives were fed poisoned leaves or hacked to death. Eventually, even old Claudius couldn't live forever. That nasty Caligula—Cousin Caligula—took over, and then old fatty Nero and his darned violin emerged, and the place went down.

There's another view, and in Gibbons' massive history, he states something like Marcus Aurelius didn't get it. You see while Rome was falling, coarsening, circling the drain, a new light started to shine. Some scruffy little Christians preached love and brotherhood and history records change and a wider unity, wider than Roman Kingdoms. Why not consider time and intervals in history, as cyclical, and consider that people of every age have a time when despite decay and decline a new Luminary, like a Divine physician appears with teachings, and heart by heart, an acceptance and awareness spreads?

Now, back where we are when we began, we, in the red states and the blue states, are not Rome. The teachers aren't the cause of the decline and fall of our world and every child is left behind. Hey, what about the teachers? They don't get on the bus either. Maybe, baby, if the world is listening, they'll hear the new news. It's not a literal end. Leave tales of dungeons and dragons to the young. We are shifting. Our equilibrium slips, lurches, as forces of dark and light dance with one another. Our story is yet to be told.

Remember the prophets and seers of yesterday and the promise of a golden time? An unfolding has come about. We are in the crucible of change as we realize our oneness and see a future where the gargoyles and ignorant armies will not clash by night. "Come what come may, time and the hour runs through the roughest day,"* and we are metaphorically back where we began, but light years ahead in our realization of humanity's coming of age. Now is the time for the ingathering of humankind. We begin again.

---

* *Macbeth*, Act I, Scene III.

Language After the 100 Year War

The Nouns were in control in the neighborhood of Verbiage. Adjectives were forced to end their 100 Year War. This war was known as the Great War of Planet Earth in the Days of Rhetoric Only. Verbiage, like a fireplace bellows of yesteryear, had simply exhausted its wheeze and could no longer control the Nation.

Politicians would no longer be described adjectively. Thus, our President could be described by the Press as, "A man whose eyes narrowed when a syllabic word entered the toy store of his mind; a man whose Rubber Ducky drowned when his bath water became higher than what is necessary for the average leader; or, a man who could bob eternally on the Ocean of Platitude."

This leader called up his country's Reserve Marines again. These Marines were sent to a land which resembled a cannon to which they would become fodder. They would obey their mission, climb into these cannons, and be shot out over the land of buildings which no longer resembled buildings. Naught would be seen but structures of rubble which resembled cookies crumbled in the hand of a monster as tall as the sky.

The Congress would not be allowed to use descriptions which included the much abused adjective. This caused some consternation, for our Congress knew of the paucity of adverbs when running for election. The Congress member would no longer be able to crawl into that vat of adjectives filled with words guaranteed to portray an individual Congress person righteously and puffily. These adjectives, I might add, are thrown carelessly into this vat, like screen plays in

Los Angeles, like potato chips in a Lays truck which had escaped from their Bag Containers.

The Nouns issued an edict: "Stick to the Facts, Jack. Straight Facts for a Straight Land," a land which had lived adjectivally and splendiferously for too long, thereby wreaking an ecological knowledge gap of a very long five years. Politicians had appeared on the NewsHour program with Jim Lehrer, and on what used to be Peter Jennings's NewsHour, and on Tim Russert, to reveal Sunday after Sunday (or was it Monday after Monday?) narrow gamboling minds and nuances of the political dance. These very same politicians verbally trolled linguistically along to thinly expand titles such as "Theatre of Operation," "War Games" and, last but not least, the most abused noun in the world, Democracy—Democracy became a gutted, slutty word, misused and stretched like hardened taffy in a candy machine after the summer crowd had gone home.

A rape of the Nouns had occurred. What choice did the Nouns have but to take over the Nation? They cried out, "Aack, aack, aack! No more." And so as this tale is difficultly told, but blessed for its attempts, all the while failing in adverbial splendor, time will tell how language controlled its environment so that facts and integrity might emerge again before the children of the world forget that "Truthfulness is the foundation of all human virtues" (*Advent of Divine Justice*, p. 62, Shoghi Effendi).

Global Soup Recipe

Lentils = Peoples of the world
Chicken broth = Your particular Faith
Water = All other core teachings from religions of the world (Zoroastrian, Hinduism, Buddhism, Judaism, Christianity, Islam, Bahá'í
Tomatoes = Ways to serve humankind
Potatoes = Prayers
Celery = Knowledge
Carrots = Volition
Onions = Action
Packaged Cream of Leek Soup = Our World Today (World Culture)
Balsamic Vinegar = Tests and Difficulties
Tamari = The unexplainable

Soak the lentils (peoples of the world) for an hour. Other instructions for lentil recipes say this is not necessary. This cook feels you should want to care for and nurture your lentils as they are making a giant leap and going into a soup with other diverse elements.

Heat chicken broth and water (yours and others' Faiths) in big pot (Earth). Immerse the lentils in the pot and bring to a boil, which in our terms is to bring to full alacrity, awareness, ability—you can supply other words if you wish—this is now your soup.

Separately sauté celery (knowledge), carrots (volition) and onions (action) together as they all need each other. One is not good without the other two. When they are bonded, blended, or a golden brown, transfer them into the soup with lentils, broth and water. Then add the tomatoes (ways to serve humankind). These tomatoes serve as a base and solidify or bring together the vegetables and lentils (giving new meaning to hot tomatoes). Next, open a package of Knorr's Cream of Leek Soup (our world culture) and shake package contents into the soup. This will give a particular tone and taste to your soup, and you can also add your own in individualized preferences of herbs and spices. Add a potato or two to permeate the whole soup and bring it together—gives it purpose so to speak.

Thirty minutes before the soup is cooked, add a quarter cup of balsamic vinegar (tests and difficulties). The soup is either close to done after an hour, or when the carrots and lentils are soft. The balsamic gives energy and texture to the soup, creates a tension of the opposites, metaphorically speaking.

Finally, add a touch of tamari, (the unexplainable), and the soup is done! There you have it: Everyone's soup. Your soup. A meal which enriches, sustains, informs, delights, and gives you purpose and vigor.

Enjoy! Call a friend, neighbor, relative, co-worker—someone you know, don't know—reach outwards and share this soup with them! *Bon appétit*!!!!

Eating Chocolate at Night

In a dark time, the eye begins to see beyond the horizons of Macy's, Trader Joe's, Peet's, and Noah's Bagels. Things have shifted. I feel it in my bones.

I am a cartoonist. I'd draw people, thin New Yorker type people, lying flat inside a Sardine Can, shoes and all. The men wear worsted suits. The women wear hats, and suits, an occasional sports outfit, and their lips are jagged red slashes against pale, bronzed, mahogany, or puce skin. I show a Giant Hand reaching out of the sky. A hairy white arm (and long fingers, hair in tufts on the fingers) moves towards the twister key on the side of the Can. It turns, and the Sardine Can tightens.

It is a dark time. I feel like a small woman without a head, but I am a large woman with a small head. How did I conjure this Sardine Can? How did I let this can crawl into my psyche? A tension of the opposites, a side door to Plato's cave, and shadow of illusion creeps into tomorrow's strip.

The Can's instructions say, "Squeeze, tighten 2006, 2007, or 200...." This can has a shelf life of a trillion years. It's right up there with packages of Susie-Q's with cream-filled chocolate cake. Then a vision of nuclear winter where no one has sweaters.

I remain a figure within the can, and I'm next to the edge. The lid descends. I can't breathe. I awaken. No more chocolates at night for me.

This is how war must feel, war which most of us don't believe in. I remember the sounds of a trillion BBs going into an empty copper barrel, representing sounds of war. People tried to show us the deafening sounds of thousands of souls annihilated.

I am in my dark eye of night, after chocolate, assessing my world. Again the dream beckons, and I am underground, down in the rabbit hole, taking a left and not a right and hearing the sound of wild wolves howling. On Friday or Sunday I will draw a strip of wolves in business suits with gray fur nesting snugly against their lapels. I will illustrate their puffing throats and their small heads and tiny brains and arms and legs as they sit in underground bunkers planning what to do after the earth quits shaking.

Boy, what a dream. It seems in the morning light, as I awaken, I'm not Mayan after all. I don't know any wolves and, mostly, I'm not a cartoonist either. I'm sick of dreaming about hard stuff like serial killers after I eat chocolate, and falling into rabbit holes of despair, food, smoking cigarettes in my dreams, wondering if my body has a big or little head. Then again I wonder about the dream's portentous aspects.

Perhaps chocolate is good?

Being Safe

Being safe is your body getting up with you, doing its thing, stretching if need be, bending if need be, and just all around running together. The toes gotta go where the feet want it because the brain is my chosen alpha organ for the day, but don't worry; tomorrow's the heart's day and then the heart remembering the brain but caring a bit more will feed you.

Kurt Vonnegut tells us to write four line poems to the end of the page which I think comes in handy.

Safe Wishes for Kurt Vonnegut.

So now, I'll wish for Anne LaMott's *Traveling Mercies* and being safe.

I'll wish the world a good warm flannel blanket in days of cold and wind, and for hot days, here's wishes for a cool breeze and lemonade without Aspartame.

"Today's the day" is every day with some days of feeling horrible, poisoned, bones pulling in, and other days when my step, old as it is buoyant, clops along to the library while my mind feels safe because I have energy, and my eyes see the delicate purple etching as jacaranda trees bloom regardless of political pundits punditing and the world following apart; I am safe for a bit.

I think we all want to be safe. Put your money where your mouth is, "I want to be safe," like the bride who wants to cement her groom's little shiny black-shoed feet into the cake, deep into white frosting, past the brown moist earth of chocolate—yeah, safe like reading the end of books, no matter, even if it's a math book, but careful, easy does it, don't want to be robotic.

Safe is the name of a film I mention at least once a year, a quiet film about a lady who feels unsafe. Julianne Moore plays a lady with allergies, environmental allergies, and she lives in California in the Valley in an expensive house, and has odd immune system responses. She finally ends up in an igloo type of building in the desert. As she stands in front of a mirror, her pale face heightens her freckles. She is alone and repeats in front of this mirror, "I love you."

I've run on for more than Kurt Vonnegut's suggested four lines, but safety isn't always staying between the lines, or sticking to the pattern, because if you were safe, would you turn the wheels of that Kaleidoscope, and see the colors, or hop on the jumper cars and go every which way, or get up in the morning, and have coffee, even though part of your heart was torn out of you because you lost some one, some thing, some concept, some, some, some, and the "somes" didn't add up to the sum of your heart's wanting to be safe.

"Safe is an inside job," you tell yourself. It's who you are inside, the one that no one sees, but gets glimmerings of, and it's your world view and your relationship to your Creator, and safe changes because the soul is always in motion, and safe risks to help others, and being safe is sacrifice on one level, because sacrifice lets go of something lower for something higher. So safe is having a net, not being without a net like some brave Circus Lady who, I might add, is trim and lithe, and if she falls, it won't be like some 500-pound Bubba out there in the neighborhood killing a sidewalk or such. No safe is reaching, trusting, like the trees in the forest with their arms up reaching to the sky; safe wants star dust and glimpses of the unseen in the daily.

Yeah, safe is feeling okay in your heart, no matter what is happening outside. Safe is a big deal. Yeah, safe, and that's what I wish for you, the reader, and for all I love, for those who struggle, labor, strive, keep us safe, and for those who fear, because courage is doing it anyhow, whether you are safe or not.

Esther's Narrow Straits

I had to go to the emergency room on 9/11 in 2006. I'm a brave little foot soldier when it comes to venturing to new lands, emergency rooms, but scratch a DMV office, and a partner's corner office in law firms.

I always grab my Bahá'í Prayers and reading material as if I were planning on studying for a doctorate when I hit the road to the hospital. Bill drives me, and calls me "kid." When things get really bad, I settle into "Esther's little death instructions." For instance, I told Margaret, "Make everybody who is at my memorial, whatever, feel included in love." I divvied up items in my mind to leave people: three volumes of Bahá'í writings to someone with a family and assured generational appreciation; my necklace with the symbol over the Shrine of Bahá'u'lláh to go to my granddaughter, who is only eight now, and verbal instructions like "play Rodrigo, blah, blah, blah." Poor Bill; he's heard this more than once.

I said "No phone calls," not because I don't love everyone, but I would use up my energy talking to so many I loved. I felt the prayers and settled for sleep around the clock, ready to look down the barrel of a gun, face my reality—new mechanical heart valve or not. Kaiser heart docs and staff are excellent. I had an echocardiogram, noninvasive, and the lady who gave it was born in Dnepropetrovsk, Ukraine, where Bill and I lived. Her father had been a Gulag survivor, and she thought *I* was brave! Needless to say, I called Bill and said, "Bring in some of my books."

I was to have a treadmill, and a possible angiogram, which would be my third. I was nervous. Have I done something wrong? Is it in my head? Am I a hypochondriac? The angiogram revealed clean, wonderful results. The guys who did it were the same ones from two years ago. I bonded with the nurses and patients, and I had a feeling that individual tests of the spiritual kind were calibrated. It turned out I have small problems with my mechanical heart valve, controllable by meds. Guess I'm like a Studebaker that goes into the garage periodically to get its tires kicked, valves checked, and ashtrays polished.

Could that be so? Calibrated Divine Love Tests? I am Chief Dodo in Math and use mathematical metaphors to explain my existence. I noticed every small event, recording small signs like the Dnepropetrovsk lady who performed my echocardiogram test said, "My father was from Dnepropetrovsk." That same day the hospital's nutritionist stopped by, and she was from a village outside of Minsk where we lived in 1992-1993.

My friend Jamie gave me a bracelet of small glossy wooden balls the size of a pea with a silver oval which read "Live." Finally I made friends with two African-American women who were giants to my puny soul. One of them was very sick. She sensed that behind our hospital curtains I was silently praying for her, and she said I would be called a "Mahvelous Sistah." God, I was grateful and honored.

This account is not meant to be a puffy piece about me, but every little sign and person seemed to be geometrically calibrated just for me, and I felt an enormous gratitude and privilege for being able at times to solace a troubled heart. I put my "live" bracelet on my roommate and said, "When you are better, pass this on to someone who needs it." She gave me her telephone number and said to call her.

Mirror Image

I see determination looking at me from the mirror. This mirror eclipses the lower portion of my body. I see a perennial question, "Who are we behind the eyes"? I see eyes finger-tipping through the world, and eyes that respond to dreams which whisper my name in the night. Then again, I see eyes which laughed at a bumper sticker, "Visualize Ballard," and to tell the truth, I see strength emerging from the delicacies of an evening ruined by an email from someone scolding my fragility of life, my "Trust in God, but tie your camel" élan.

I see generations of Irish, those people I disparaged in my younger mind's eye, those people who as they age look like Beagles against brushed velvet. I see my Irish genetics and heredity carve out its claim, pushing cultural influence aside.

I see a woman with a sadness which smells like tin, hammered, punctured with dents, and emotions raw as a child's scraped knee, but don't tell your parents, because only the lectures follow, and I see courage and a straight back, and a willingness to look down gun barrels and see blossoms of flowers at the end.

I see tears in my throat, sliding over my heart. These tears form a thin veil of water, caught in the sunlight, against a heart which feels like concrete. I see what used to be a bruised peach pit centered in my heart, but now capable of holding no grudge.

I remember *Who is Writing the Future?*, and I remember Ukrainian train rides at four o'clock in the morning, and I remember crawling across train tracks lugging books. I remember cookies and then talks about *Who is Writing the Future?* as I traveled through Eastern Ukraine with my interpreter who was a Tartar, but more than a Tartar, a soul sister.

And now, with the smell of a tuna sandwich and someone preparing lunch, I realize this was the week to work on old things, others' issues, others' scolding. I feel a deliberation and purpose arise like an enfolding circular staircase within, climbing to the top of the sky, and I might pleat the moon in gratitude for a friend's visit, but I would never undress this moon. No, my New England standards scream modesty.

I see someone who misses a pug and what about a pug who could sing *La Boheme*? But then again, a warm smell of wheat toast filters the air, and I will eat Ralphs' Grocery tuna, tart, crispy. Bill is fixing lunch, and I feel his love fill these rooms. I know that I will never hate, because hate tastes like eating old peeling paint. I will taste, though. I will also learn not to retain hurt, because retaining hurts seems like taking a medicine which pulls the tongue into curls and feels like an old dead tree. Going beyond this hurt will turn into fields of flowers and rainbows. Ultimately, I see wisdom, a rainbow of incandescence and radiance, and I realize, this is just a glimpse of a soul after a rough week.

For Liz, a Remembrance of Things Past—First Bout of Cancer (April 2006)

I felt like a large toy barge, beached on a sandbar, as fine riverboats glided by, I watched, frozen in space and time. My husband and I stayed in Idaho, near the cows, underneath clouds that crawled across the sky like long, low-slung crocodiles.

I felt like a mineral immersed in acid. My thoughts were nepheline in formation. Bill and I wanted to transform my twin Liz, who lay ten pounds lighter in the time we had been there. She was not skeletal when we first arrived in her small town of Caldwell. Towards the end of radiation treatments she could barely drink a spoonful of water. She would lie under the covers not moving, huddled under a blanket and comforter, waiting for the end of weeks of radiation. "We are caretakers. We are not miracle workers," Bill reminds me.

I remembered tales of Liz and our baby days when we were the Bradley twins, born twelve minutes apart in the Boston Lying-in Hospital. She was the chubby one and went home immediately, while I, second born with four pounds clinging to my bones, remained in the hospital to fatten up. We had similar characteristics, but were opposites, like bookends, each reflecting our own dimensions. She played sports, climbed trees, and finally in the third grade liked reading, because the book *Eddie and His Fire Engine* turned her on.

I was thin, dark, and given to squinting and looking out at the world with mistrust. I read constantly, and roller-skated and jumped rope. I was last to be called for softball teams, or anything else for that matter. Liz was first. She was the twin who saved her ice cream, licked small, tidy laps, while I, the greedy one, gobbled mine ahead.

As life evolved, we became polar opposites.

Her second husband died of bone cancer, and she moved to Idaho for a safe place to raise young children. She had her children late, starting at forty-two. I had my son ten years earlier. She was never sick, but at nineteen she had been in a major accident with brain stem injury. I was constantly battling immune system viruses.

Where she was contained, reserved, and had studied well in high school and in nursing school, I was outgoing beyond measure, with a reserve quotient of nil. I had been a discipline problem in my early years of high school. One teacher referred to us as "the good twin and the bad twin." Liz and I were close at times and then would spend years distanced from one another.

In my forties, I went back to school, to college. I was divorced and a single mom; she was married with a small child. She didn't' approve of my going to college. Finally she understood.

She became closer to our father in his later years. He had remarried after our mother had died. I was afraid of him. They were emotionally the same, and I was like our mother, not a good reminder to my father. Still, despite our differences, Liz and I always responded to calls of help from each other.

I married in 1985, and I had been a Bahá'í for twenty years. This belief bothered her. She took Bill aside and basically implied we were doomed. Bill thanked her, and we just continued connecting. I felt at one point all we could talk about were the dogs. "How are the dogs?" The number varied from two to five. "How are the kitties?" I would send her animal cards that made her laugh. Hers was a religion which said "only"—but her illness bumped "only" to the back of the room.

Liz's cancer was an aggressive and rare cancer. Luckily, radiation caught it all, and her nodes were clean. I wondered about the environment. Idaho has a lot of farm land, and planes spray the crops with pesticide. Her well water was good, but other sections of the city were notified by the state of nitrates.

Bill went away for several weeks while I stayed with Liz. This was at the beginning of our time together. It was difficult.

I walked, prayed, walked, prayed, and cooked small morsels of food. I wondered, how does one render Carnation Instant Breakfast Drink exquisite? There's more to this story, as pages will reveal. I witnessed hers and others' suffering at the cancer clinic, but I also felt a thin, gray line pulled Liz and me together. I labeled that line "love." Yes, I think it was love, and love made us laugh and use cows and warts on noses, the ugly things, to discover within the ordinary everything is beauty.

Invisible Traveler

One early morning at the Caldwell Cancer Center, I sit at the guest computer pushing the s, l, j, k letters all the while my mind's eye recalls the Caldwell cows grazing on a hill near the Cancer Center. This morning they stood pointing east. They were stolid, staring, and unmoving.

I am like a Caldwell cow; mute, invisible. I note things here at the Cancer Center—a place where my twin and I end up, again sharing, as we shared ten comic books we received as a joint birthday present, or the one Parcheesi game, another joint gift. It's easy, this sharing, thinking about the cows out there feeding, thinking of the cows as having haiku coats.

Does laughter roll over their hides? Do they compete for attention with Idaho's very own Simplot potato? Their thoughts of moo and chew float through me, allowing me to just be, not think, not feel, and be invisible.

We are all Invisible Travelers, and yet I must dare to give voice to thoughts, to soul pettiness and soul triumphs, both endured and revealed in a day. My soul is getting wider; hips steady, remain the same. So it goes, near the cows, near the brave people sitting quietly inside this Center in chairs, well cushioned. These gray faces record nothing but patience. We connect to one another on this thread of patience: the cows, my sister, the patients.

Am I There Yet?

Am I there yet? I read books like *Bleak House*—thick book, poundage noted on back, 500 pages to skim and not get hot thick chocolate sauce on the wafer thin pages. Scan quickly, go, jump, hop, see Jane run, look Dick, Spot moves away. Moving, constantly moving, on the way to the Land of There.

Yesterday (meaning Biblical time—yes, let's give one day a thousand years), when Liz and I were teenagers, and then young adults, and then married with children, I was skinny, tired, frightened, apologizing to the clouds overhead because I was in their way. I didn't dare speak about meaningful things, didn't dare form my voice. I wondered how life could be so interminably long within the walls of law firms, down long corridors where mostly women sat in partitioned cubby holes typing, as if pushing cloth through ancient sewing machines. There seemed no way out.

I no longer feel like a moth with the windows sealed inside a clean white modern building, where carpet grabbed my feet to make me silently steal steps and hoof in an ambient rush. Now I am out there. There is what I call "surfing the opaque waves," dealing with the laundry machinery of the outer world and my inner stuff. So most of the time, I am there. I am not afraid of my own voice anymore.

Is it okay to speak? You bet your sweet bippy it is. I am present, in the moment, which moments include time in a house in Caldwell, Idaho, near some cows, amongst the nitrates of cow country and golf courses. These nitrates are rotting out the electric wires in some tract housing. I am there with my twin who is dying.

Funny being an old twin. Cute when you are six, holding hands, squinting up at the sun, innocent, free of dark knowledge. Now, with more miles on my psyche and at an age where whispers of wisdom visit me every now and then, like a cousin who likes my Hot Chocolates, I've signed up for the state of "Being Here."

I'm not waiting to become a ballerina on the New York stage so I can hear the sound of my hoofs. I'm just ready to stand in the moment, the ones I have left, and look square in the face of whatever is happening.

In Pasadena, I listened to Dr. Joy DeGruy Leary's recorded talk about Post Traumatic Slave Syndrome, and I wrote a piece called "Children of the Stolen Ones." But every now and then some psychic force picks me up by the back of my neck or my thatched hair and transplants me very quickly to a new place, a new culture, and flat spaces spread out before me with surreal speed where I am to adapt to here. I have lived in seventeen different places and lived in Ukraine and traveled to Siberia, but I have never been in the space I am now.

I am in a new flat space, taking care of my twin sister, who is curled up like a small dog, under covers, dozing, hoping for an end to the nine weeks of radiation, nausea, pain, gray face, no appetite. She shrinks into a small question mark, determined to hang in, using strong spiritual resources. Before I came here, I knew I was to be in this country of cows and big trucks with library books holding more than one Bible name. I knew I was at a place in my life where I just was going to stand up and look down the barrel of a gun if necessary

For someone who once was a four-pound baby, afraid of everything, even knotholes in pine walls, and a father's voice, and later, white men in corner offices, this is good. I am just here. I'm traveling with my soul, and just hoofing. Isn't that what it's about?

Waiting For Bad News—Second Bout of Cancer

The wind in the tall field grass in Caldwell, when the sun is going down, sounds like an "oooohhhhh," a howling, empty sound, suggesting bad news. Mostly when I walk, I am soothed by this sound. The wind both settles and unsettles me, not unlike being in Caldwell, walking past tidy houses and mostly vast fields. I feel existential loneliness and a time of mystic questioning as I hoof up a high road, ignoring barking dogs and horses grazing.

Liz is resting, and Bill is with her. My mix of feelings reminds me that to Bill, I am his Dolly With a Hole In Her Stocking. He asked me one day what did I mean, "I feel existential loneliness"?

Existential loneliness also means when I go to the Hollywood Bowl, I feel empty because there are too many people, and I don't know them. That's when I feel angst and a longing for quiet tall grass to cover me up from parking lots, freeways, and picnic boxes and box seats, too wide and empty.

I walk while Bill, Matt, and Lindsey are with Liz. She is Elizabeth to them, and these past few days have been totally rough. I want Liz to be released, but this waiting time reminds me of one winter day in December in Boston. It was a major day of waiting.

We were in shock. Our mother was in a hospital because of a massive cerebral hemorrhage. We had moved to Back Bay, a part of Boston, to Bay State Road, right next to Boston University's Sheldon Hall, a girls' dormitory. Our apartment went from the front sidewalk all the way back to an alleyway. We were on the top floor which overlooked an esplanade, by the Charles River. College teams crewed on this river, and in December, when the wind was icy and went straight through us, we walked our Pug and Boxer.

We moved from a twelve-room house to make things easier on our mom physically. Our high school was still in our old neighborhood, and it took over an hour to get to our new home in Back Bay. Liz hopped on the trolley earlier, and I came home several hours later. Liz found our mom lying on the floor beside her bed. Mom was unconscious. She called our dad, and an ambulance came. When I got home, Dad was with Mom, and Liz was alone.

The family mantra, was "No news is good news," so we waited, and waited. We were hanging out in our living room, which was spacious and had big windows looking out at the Charles River. We were restless and sat at the piano and banged some ancient simplistic tunes out, and then we watched Arthur Godfrey. A surreal numbness stung our bones until our dad came home and said, "She's gone."

Now in Idaho, I am reminded that waiting for bad news is like having a taffy machine pulling and stretching those lovely ice cream colors of candy—pale greens, light pinks, banana yellows—until suddenly the machine jerks and spasms, and dark, dark twisted candy spits out.

Waiting for bad news makes me feel like I am inside a huge tent where the worst is supposed to happen. I fold up and become terrorized. I don't move and wonder if I'll ever breathe again. I'll tell you one thing, though: I used to wait for bad news, expect bad news, but now I just show up at life, go to the plate and bat the ball. When facing the uglies, bad news isn't always bad news. It can be a death of some aspect of self, and it sucks and feels awful from one point of view. I think our Creator sends a posse across the sky, and invisible things start to happen. Real people show up, and somehow invisible hands support me. I become still and just face what I have to face, and after bad news comes good news; and after good news comes not-so-hot news; and after not so-hot-news comes...whatever.

It's dark now, and I am soothed. The sound of the wind is softer against the grass, almost as if a melody of muted notes plays softly. Somewhere I sense the smell of sweet grass in a meadow and know some day I'll rejoice over sweet grass and dark and light moments.

Being on Watch—Second Bout With Cancer (Spring 2007)

What day do I run to? Does my twin Elizabeth think of this? Her body is a mere cipher. She's buying the farm. How do I run to her call, "Help me, help me, help me," which starts just after dawn and carries through the day and night? I jolt out of bed at 5:30 and run into her room, a two-second trip. Early mornings and late evenings require me, her twin. No one else can help at the moment. Bill covers the ritual of medicine doses, and Lindsey and Matthew—her son and his wonderful wife—are going to start staying over.

Liz worries about my dying alone. "Who will you have?" I reassure her, and then I fantasize my demise. I would not realize this was a religious choice reference—that she feared my acceptance of Bahá'u'lláh would hold me back. At the time, I laughed and said, "I'll be fine."

I always said, "I want to go out lying on a huge bed with hundreds of pug dogs over me, as I feebly say, "Put the last one on that space over my nose above my lips." So under a snuff and snort, I'd end my days. Strange is this getting older.

This is going to be an essay. I feel it in my bones. Tonight, my words slough off this day of sitting next to Liz, trying to get hourly liquids into her.

I sit in her kitchen at the computer which makes its "Urr-urr" noises, like a new baby. It's quiet in the kitchen as I reflect on our life as twins. Now, we are beyond the personalities of our twin selves. We are finally down to what really matters. Like Liz, I am waiting to return home, except it's not my time, and I'm still on earth duty, in dirt city, on Planet Earth. I want to go home to Pasadena.

Today someone in the writing group posted a question, "What day do I run to?" What does that mean? Then I thought, this is one of my middle-of-the-night questions when I get up and think, when does it end? I, always the frailer twin, have survived heart surgeries and other stuff.

It helps at night to sit in her kitchen at the computer and play with writing prompts from our CHPerc site for writers. The basic question is, "Where do I run?" "When do I run out?" Did I tread the mystical path on practical feet? Did I hoof hard? Was I a solace? Now, it's just enough to realize, parts of me are like a big old watch. On what day will I stop ticking? Will it be 2:00 in the afternoon or 2:00 at night? Where will the world be then? Meanwhile, I'm on watch, and I'm writing.

Here in Liz's kitchen on a quiet Idaho night, I think of us, Liz and me. We were the survivors. We've always had each other—like book ends. My brother John has been missing for years, and my older sister (Meb, for Mary Ellen Bradley) died at fifty. Liz and I were it.

Meb was a Girls Latin Scholar and later an unwed mother. "Go tell Dad, he'll understand," backfired, and she was sent away. She had the baby by herself in Quincy Hospital, but then, as she turned eighteen, she took her baby out of foster care. She married her young love and had three more kids. Her husband left her, so she became a pianist in cocktail lounges. She drank too many drinks offered by grateful customers standing by her piano in a club lounge. Life unraveled, and she ended up on the streets, in housing tenements, dying in a hospital, the same Quincy Hospital where she gave birth. She was alone, poor, alcoholic, and had emphysema.

When my twin and I were seventeen, our mom died. I remember Liz and I taking the trolley into downtown Boston and answering the sales lady's query, "Why do you have to have black dresses?" My father later remarried. He said to me, when I was forty and my son was about ten, "Don't write your children off as I did."

My twin is the essence of "don't tell," and she never discusses feelings about family. She would tell me during last year's radiation treatments. When she was ten, standing in our long, graveled driveway, she said to herself, "I'm on my own now. I have to take care of myself." My mother's alcoholism had burst out. The Twelve Steps programs were not as known, and the doctors would send our mother to a private sanatorium for shock treatments. And what about us, Liz and me? She was the sturdy one, good at sports, tree climber par excellence, devotee of "Bobby and the B-Bar Ranch" radio show and "Sgt. Preston" and his dog King. And me—softy, wimp, reader, reader, reader, pathfinder of all the childhood diseases—feeling my mother's pain. Our early lives had a Dvorak dissonance, later transiting to the spiritual sound of "Coming Home."

As I await my twin's death, I want to tell you it's a symphony, this life. First, the sacred wounds inflicted upon the soul, and time and twists and colors and sounds, cymbals, drums, some bells and whistles of the funky kind. And the colors—fuchsia, black, gray, stripes of every hue and finally the color blue, a Mediterranean blue—an embracing veil of silken color, obliterating memories of my twin's despair of my believing in more than Jesus. Also fading are the memories of criticism's early work. I hope when it comes my time to pass—come to a reckoning, a passage into a final exam, a leap of gladness, the warrior path almost finished—that I be worthy to meet my Creator. I think before I go, I'll give a final glance at a world back from tilt and furor, and I'll catch faint sounds of a new symphony, an oratorio, celebrating unity and splendor for the human race.

Penciling In July 2007

I should have known I was a downright obsessive kid back then on Wren Street, when I'd gather my dimes, pennies, and walk a half an hour to the ten cent store to buy paper clips. Paper clips—buy them, and hook them together in a long chain. In my kid days, I wanted to hook a chain up to the sky. The more clips I hooked together, the better the hopscotch throw, and the better chances I'd land on a top number.

Now in a body that doesn't hop as it used to, I've forgotten the layout of hopscotch, but not the intensity and quietness of an early evening on Wren Street as Liz, Ruthie Anderson and I played hopscotch, ignoring mugginess and mosquitoes. I've forgotten the games Liz and I played, incessant competition of twins moving quickly from one game or adventure to another.

A month ago Liz died. I realize I am at the "pencil this in" stage of life. Themes of impermanence and movement merge. I still throw items at squares and hop to them in a "Calendar Your Days Gal" sort of way. I go where I am called. This time it was Caldwell, Idaho, where I penciled addresses, people, directions and telephone numbers to my mind like loose Velcro strips.

We've been on the go in our twenty-one years of marriage. In fact, we've lived in seventeen different places which gives "pencil this in" new tones and inky meanings. All of it is like landing on hopscotch squares, this time a square indicating "love's labor is never lost." That's a quote from someone, and as soon as I get off shooting the breeze here, I'm going to query that quote.

Google soothes my psyche's brain, feeds the pseudo-librarian's "check on that right away" persona. I was raised to jump quickly and readily sprint forward, but last month's jump was a leap. No competitive throwing of the world's best chain of paper clips, but a readied presence by my sister's bed.

Sixty-eight years of knowing each other seems like such a brief span of time. Her final gift, as she lay on her side, bald, thin, wide-eyed, quieted by morphine, was a phrase, "I never realized how you were always there for me." I'd like to think our souls met. Her expectations of my not being of a certain political party, a certain religious faith, a certain weight, not a lover of Wal-Mart, nor devotee of the conservative radio programs—these expectations fell away. I, too, didn't care who she voted for to be president or put a yellow Ten Commandments sign on her lawn or made innuendos about my chunkiness. The important was discarded for the most important. My relief was palpable. I replied, "I love you," and she replied, in her sweet grave manner, "I love you too." That moment summed up our twinness and sent our battles, fights, stealing clothes behind each other's back, squabbles about boyfriends, who had the television clicker, who is going to sit in the front seat, and "Mother loves me more than you," to fields of oblivion.

Love's labor has a way of crawling and twisting, and at our final bend of path together, personalities dissolved. I knew I was solidly standing on a good hopscotch square. This phrase so quietly and formally uttered by her to me was no lightly penciled recording, but a silver etching clearing away minor grief, a tribute to love's labor.

Unbroken Line (June 2007)

My sister's hand was pale, and her forearms moist. What's it like for a twin to be witness to a birth, the birth at the end of time here in earth school, not a gallery, but a workshop?

She had ceased breathing while I sat at my computer in her kitchen, exhausted from a month's witnessing her agitation, lucid thoughts, holding her in my arms, doing student nurse type of things like learning to hammer out crushed ice, with the ice in any kind of clean towel we could grab from the kitchen and hurry back to her. Her body in the end was luminous, but she had stopped breathing, and a body no matter how beautiful, simply does not tell you reliable truth about the soul who had just left.

A few months earlier, I had been witness to the doors of Weimar, Germany, with pictures of my dear young friends, pictures of doors of Bach's hometown, cobblestone streets, and a restaurant with beefy beef and potatoes which split apart from a quivery touch of a fork or spoon. But then there were the doors of houses in Caldwell, Idaho.

These doors were open and spilling out casseroles with a bit of creamed this or creamed that. The neighborhood cooks kept up a steady supply of feeding our little group of four as we took care of Liz. My nephew Matt, and his wife, dear Lindsey, and Bill and I were assistants and trainees, under guidance from the hospice team.

Elizabeth (always Liz to me) and I were connected by an unbroken line. That line was tested over the years. I may have alluded that fraternal twins are not like identical twins. But I had to remind myself at times. We think different feelings, thoughts. Identical twins think the same thoughts, feel the same feelings, and utter the same cries.

But, the fact is the line wasn't broken, and while she stayed in Caldwell, and I twitted about the world a wider piece, the line did its job, staying firm or loose or taut, but still a line. The line has dissolved into space unknown, a silver blue thing of mystical origins. And now I, a traveler in the fractal worlds of God, think of her in random moments of my day in wonder of the doors that lie ahead of her.

Pieces of Soul (June 18, 2007)

I wanted to be with Liz when she died. She was close to passing and her body produced short gasps—so many breaths a minute. I wasn't in her room, because I had to go and totally rewrite the essay for her eulogy because I thought it was lousy. I didn't see her as ready to go. So maybe it was good. Matt, her son, held her hand, while he read her last words, her goodbye letter to her firstborn. Matt read these words out loud, and then he turned away and left the room to cry. He came back seconds later. No breath came from Liz. We all ran to her room. I gazed at her: her head pale, blotchy, bald, mouth open, quiet, gone, someone I've known for every minute of my life.

A piece of my soul went with her. Parts of me have been like a platoon of army ants, working with Matt, and Lindsey and Bill, 24/7 duty. Hospice guided us. My part was to help my sister die, to feel loved and cared for. She had to go beyond her utter distress that my beliefs were not her beliefs. We played a lot of music for her, and the nightly playing of *Ave Maria* particularly quieted her agitation. I held her a lot, and Matt and Lindsey were tireless in their support as the days swept together.

Some days she was ceaselessly restless, twisting at twenty minute intervals, trying to leave her bed. She'd cry out, "Help me, help me." Then there came some quieter times when friends visited and held her hand a lot. The hardest person I have ever loved died, and a month of round-the-clock hey-let's-get-this-kid-tucked-in, fell away. Did I say I think hospice workers should be bronzed and made into statues in the park? Four Rivers Hospice and Margaret and Tess and, and,

and. These wonderful hospice people made our lives sane by their celestial support and patience.

Our memory's history—Liz and I, with a history of tricycles, kindergarten days, double knit red mittens, hand knit, red cable knit sweaters, our history of Ballroom Dancing School, blackout curtains, sharing Parcheesi games, fighting over Monopoly, arguing over who sits in the front seat, and squabbling who would get an ice cream cone first. We remembered when margarine was invented and what it felt like to wear roller skates and tighten them up with a key and feel a smooth, black sidewalk rolling underneath us.

So, in this time as I molt into a non-twin state, I am grateful to be here. Reptilian hurts left a long time ago. It's a palimpsest, this soul growth. In days before paper was used, parchment was written upon. This parchment passed through generations, each parchment having new writing or symbols placed upon the old. It gives new meaning to ancestral connectedness, archetypal views.

Old judgments no longer imprint my soul, only moments of viewing the final ascent. It's not so hard after all, and yet it's very hard. "Seesaw, Marjorie Daw," comes to mind as I think of our many moments on the highest seesaw in the black asphalt playground of our youth. Time for both of us to let go.

The Color of Death

Death ain't what you thought it would be, baby. It would be varied and graded like all us creatures in the world—shades of gray, metric black and white.

If death were a color it would be a rainbow, with the black starting first so as not to surprise the newly transported soul who is in for a notice of change. What's wrong with, "This is the only way"? Nope, it wouldn't have an only one-way color; and it would taste like medicine at first, but it would be like riding the Ferris Wheel higher than ever before.

If death were a feeling, it would be like my tummy going on a big bump, jumping up high inside, but skipping down in delight and finding out not all bumps are meant to hurt, and give new meaning to bumped up. Yep, bumped up to the higher realms of intricate oneness.

Death would feel light and like bouncy, bouncy bally, a verse uttered by nine-year-olds in school yards past, and it would be as sturdy as a red rubber ball in a school yard and smell sort of rubbery, familiar like with maybe a touch of vanilla, because vanilla soothes the senses, don't you know?

And inside, the smell would make me feel just oh, so safe, and if death were a sound, it would be echoes of kids in ages past shouting out beyond the sky, the stars, and the moon, Olly olly oxen free...ready or not, here I come."

Lobbing

wimbledon plays, bop, pop, british accents
i sorrow for a twinging tooth
wimbledon plays, bop, pop, british accents
a back tooth like an old couch waiting for Goodwill

sorrow was two weeks ago standing in front of
my twin's coffin, she in her blue bridal dress of old
me, alive, sorrowing for the little girl on a tricycle
sorrowing for her life of dripping Rorschach ink

wimbledon plays, bop, pop, british accents
sorrow has gone up like a balloon on a helium sortie
wimbledon plays, bop, pop, british accents
thwatting away epic events tumbling through and around
the people on the earth's stage

order, thwats, pops, bops, all metronome-like
in their reassurance, the steadied beat of routine
comfort, sorrow, joy, laughter, anger, all runs together
wimbledon plays, bop, pop, british accents

Horse Piss and Rotted Straw[*]

Horse piss and rotted straw, reader. I am still in my utilitarian nightgown. This nightgown is peach, salmon, with turquoise coffee cups and pots against a blue background—make that faded blue—with it's own recordings of stains, and has little words in spidery black script that say, "Ahhhhh, love my coffee." It is late morning. We are in reentry, having been away for several months because of serious family matters.

So I went to Idaho, thinking in my spare time—other than caring for my sister and gazing at the Caldwell Cows—that I would walk the country roads six miles a day. I forgot that neighbors' casseroles resplendent with cream this or cream that, and my nephew's ice cream stash with invisible siren calls, would beckon parts of my body, like Greedy Mouth auditioning for a morality play.

One day I walked in the heat of the day, which was over 100 degrees, and I took pictures of the magic of farm machines doing the integral work of getting the hay off the ground, sort of like getting my ass... oh, I digress. Then I became housebound as Liz—Elizabeth to everyone else, but my twin, Liz—succumbed to a rampant cancer. She was first born of the two of us, and I am glad I was there to help and see her on her way. I write more about her in other pieces.

We are back, having eaten our way home. We'd get up at six and drive until we were too tired to continue in the heat and stop at motels and head for big main meal lunches around three or four o'clock. Now, back in Pasadena, we are surrounded by buddies whose main passion is Twohey's in Al-

---

[*] James Joyce, *Portrait of an Artist as a Young Man*.

hambra, with their massive sundaes in huge, thick clear-stemmed glasses.

The waiter said, "Is that all I can get you?" I said, "The moon would be nice," and he said "How?" I said, "Well don't pleat it, but whipped cream and fudge sauce would tickle the palate." Bill and Johnnie were chin deep in their sundaes when our waiter brought me a chocolate-and-M&M cookie, which had whipped cream a story high on it and delicate etchings of chocolate syrup. I ate it with grace, and thought, should I tell everyone I am getting out of jury duty because of heart disease?

The doctor signed the "Excused From Jury" form, so I decided not to tell him we have been whining and then dining with friends who insist that "just this once, have the special Cheese Frittata," and "just this once, do this."

Well, many a mickle macks a muckle, and I am in a body pickle. Today is an oh-frabjous day, where time and the hour run through its suggested roughest day, where reality sets in, and I get to clean the house; clean the this, the that, and my pit vipers sit in formation on my head and hiss at me for my Craven Ways. Today is the day before the day of reckoning.

Thought I'd say today is the day of reckoning. Nope, I just made oatmeal in a healthy attempt to establish a new clean relationship with my arteries, and the top of the container sealed over the microwave bowl as if a football helmet was cemented on a key player, and I would not be allowed any of that. Was it the universe speaking to me, chiding me for my solipsistic indulgent ways?

Read and Sung

Do not ask of your shadow's future. Do not dwell on your shadow's past. Do not ask what others think. Rely not upon the delusions of the many. Do not turn away from certitude and a multisyllabic path. Do not listen to politicians' rhetoric. Do not become a sleeping mute, a junk yard dog. Do take yourself and shadow on a dual path. Take a soul to lunch this week. Better yet, take your soul with you. Best yet, be your soul.

Having My Druthers

If I had my druthers about being another person, it wouldn't be a mud flap girl, proud of my rear parts and body, represented as a "silhouette" on the dark, dark flaps of trucks moving Miller's Draft Beer, stopping in a San Bernardino Truck Stop where the air hangs heavy and super-sized Cokes swim towards reptilian brains.

Nope. I'd be like my Uncle Bill Johnson, who wasn't really my Uncle Bill Johnson, who visited us every week and wrote letters and wrote a poem about our dog being made of bones and meat with head and tail on either end and neatly wrapped in skin and hair. I'd draw cartoons and miniature figures, a combination of whimsy, verse, art, causing adults to lay down on the floor and clutch their sides laughing. I'd sort of have a James Thurber, E.B. White side of me, and whimsy would be like a mosquito netting covering my psyche.

I would eat the sun. No, I would eat words about the sun, trillions and billions and skillions of words about the sun. I'd tan and shrink to a charcoal briquette, and like Icarus go splot into the ether. Icarus' wings melted. I would briquette out. Either way is extinction.

Was I a whisper on the stairs, conceived with a twin who said, "I'm going out first. You have to wait." Did I begin my journey, moving towards the Unknowable Essence, metaphorically parallel to moving towards the sun? Was I hardwired to know and to love my Creator?

I know now that faith is conscious knowledge, and that knowing and loving qualities express themselves into action. I know now that words can never wrap around loving this Ancient Force, this Creator, but knowing and loving will be enhanced by recognizing the Prophets, the Divine Luminaries, the Manifestations, and learning the attributes of God. It's a highly personal journey, and this Creator is closer to us than our life's vein.

I found out the physical world has its divine counterparts. Lordy, how can an old girl who flunked Geometry and slept through 3rd Year Algebra twice, explain this? You can't ever know the essence of the Sun. Okay, I get that, but boys and girls, I can learn the attributes of the sun. So, let me see, that means my soul receives its light from the Sun, which is the Creator, whose essence is unknowable. I can understand the attributes of my soul, and understand attributes of my Creator by learning the Word of God. I think that boils down to, there's no yellow brick road lit up with a straight "go here from there" sign.

That's where I am today in my understanding. I do know this. I wouldn't choose to live in any time but now, because would I have been brave enough, strong enough to live in earlier days? Nope. I think my small contributions and large quests belong right here in the here and now. So that's the door to another world, the world of the inner journey, the collective process, the tension of the opposites. Everything, everything, is grist for the mill.

Packing for the Future

If you had to pack a suitcase for the next world, what would you pack for that Great Conveyor Belt in the Sky? All your earthly things would be Velcroed to the outside of your suitcase, and would fall off.

Inside this suitcase, you could put in all the good things you've done in your life but you can't take the bad things. Sure, recount them, but you won't be using any bad tools like: backbiting; not being truthful; hating someone; ignoring the sorrow-stricken, poverty-stricken—all that sort of stuff.

You see, somebody's up there writing on a Tablet of Chrysolite as you go through Life Review, with your thimble full of good or a bucket. None of us know what our capacity is. Maybe your quota was thimble-sized, and wouldn't that be a relief? You know, I was a very small baby, and that's what I used to think: "Probably, I'm only thimble capacity."

Of late, I think, hmmmm, you never were good in math, maybe it's more that's expected from me. So when I get to that Great Big Beyond, the Worlds of God, and in My Father's House there are many mansions, God willing and the crik don't rise, I'll know what kind of a being of light I'll be. Hope I'm not a dot on the blip of the entrance to Hitler's soul or 20 billion leagues under the mezzanine level of Dante's Inferno. I'd rather be near floodlights of light like Frederick Douglass, Thomas Merton, Etty Hillesum, Dorothy Baker, Enoch Olinga, and a forever list.

I would definitely leave my body on the outside, puffy old thang. Puffy old thang, I think I love you, Puffy Old Thang. I try to match my voice to the song, "Wild thing, Wild thing, I think I love you." I would reluctantly leave my earth trips for ice cream at Rite Aid for the double scoop of Pecan and Praline, on a sugar cone, tipped over in a small round carton, plastic spoon in beginning excavation stage on left side of said carton. I would leave my dodo-ness of geometry, algebra, becoming a discipline problem in 6th grade sewing class when we made big gym bloomers of blue that had elasticized leg bands, and I would leave behind on the planet the Gargoyle Boys, with souls of stone, planning the next Theatre of War. I would also leave all language suggesting violence but clothed in football or MBA terms.

It would be good to make the handles of my suitcase firm, and let someone help me/get someone to help me carry the innards, each handle shared, one in my hand and the other in a friend's hand, like in Russia. In the next world, I think cooperation is the name of the game. I'd carry photos of all the people in Russia and America and India and poverty-filled neighborhoods, here right up the street in Pasadena, and the photos showing beginnings of reading circles, and after-school programs, and meals and child care provided to moms who are screaming with generational and post traumatic slave syndrome pain.

Finally, I would carry words like solace and hope, and I would have the biggest picture of my African-American sisters and brothers, because they are like the Pupil of the Eye, and they are not victims, but noble, and their suffering has put their souls leagues away from me. I think in the next world they will be "the chosen ones." In that next world, if I am so lucky, I am going to apply for a position as serf or helper to serve them and learn of their qualities of patience and creativity. And maybe I'll learn to sing a bit and use warm colors and always be supportive and loving in an audience and, above all, learn how in God's name my beloved brothers and sisters from the Pupil of the Eye group—the ones that see so clearly—how they manage or did manage to keep such loving laughter within their buoyant beings, beings of such magnitude. So goes this small writing which started out as a hey,

hey, olly olly oxen free, where is everyone, come out and play, and now into a prose poem honoring the most honorable.

The Language of God

The language of God transcends syllables and sounds. It is not silken robes and incense swung in earthen jars. It is not a belief in the Divine which divides into a dance of ritual and self-obsession. It is the revitalization of the atom at the beginning of every Revelation. It is the progression of man marking mankind's gradual coming of age. It is far away from the ken of humankind and yet closer than our life's vein.

The language of God is visible in a five-year-old of ebony skin who sits on a tricycle, on a black asphalt top, near an apartment with boards on the window as she announces at evening's ebb, in a voice tinged with determination and a shred of astonishment: "Some day I am going to be a woman." The language of God translates in this day to service, and how long, oh my God, do we let agonies of poverty and race continue?

The language of God is not a radio talk show where rhetoric divides, or a preacher filling a stadium with "I talked to God today." The language of God, like an arrowhead, penetrates the unsuspecting heart. The language of God doesn't pick and choose spirituality at the quantum physics checkout stand. The language of God does not promote wars between two tribes so lost to the essential verities of religion, lost to their mutual descent, their common ancestry from the line of Abraham.

The language of God is: a tear running down someone's face; a pilgrimage to solace a broken heart; a poem on a blank page; Rodrigo's "Concierto de Aranjuez," which vaults, twists, and wraps around my soul, calling to mind the deep, deep blue colors I call 'Akká Blue to remind me of the holy places in Haifa.

"The language of God is love," the poet Marina Tsvetayava said, but she added, "Beyond that love is the poet's pain." The language of God is the writer Etty Hillesum, able to see the barracks at Westerbork lie "like a forgotten object in the silvery moonlight," as she determined to love harder and know there was a greater age to come. The language of God lies in the Hopi prophecies, the poet's page, the fluted note, the commingling of science and religion's station. The language of God is creation and oneness, and recognition of essential verities at the core of every religion, the obsolescence of blind imitation.

The language of man has been one of struggle, attainment and now on our horizon, horrendous abuse—but the language of God is stamped upon my puny soul, within which "myriad universes are enfolded." A prisoner in 'Akká, "the Most Great Beauty, the Comforter, the Redeemer, the Divine Physician, the Glory of the Lord, the King of Glory," spoke these words:

> "…these fruitless strifes, these ruinous wars shall pass away and the Most Great Peace shall come. Is not this that which Christ foretold? Let not a man glory in this, that he loves his country; let him rather glory in this, that he loves his kind."*

The language of God watches mankind play, like stunted gargoyles, with forces of light and darkness. Darkness seems visible at noon, but consider darkness as absence of light. A monosyllabic word, *light*, beckons us all to a foretold promise of World Peace. The catch is, peace is promised, attainable, certifiably true. The trick is to avoid barbaric action, reptilian imitation, and seek out language's new path of *consultation*, seek out consultative will amongst the people. So, if darkness is absence of light, and evil is an absence of good, and hate an absence of love, and Love is a cohesive force, then beauty lies in syllabic promises, "be brave," "have courage," "we are

---

* Introduction to *A Traveller's Narrative* (Episode of the Bab), pp. xxxix-xl.

one," and the "Most Great Peace shall come." Time and its properties, on the other hand, is another totally different discussion.

Pilgrimage—Bahá'í Shrines
(March 2007)

What exactly was it I did hear in those silent moments where time and the soul—my soul, to be exact—took a ride to another dimension and time flattened out, and I stepped with measured gait towards the Threshold of the Blessed Beauty calling to mind, "The Ancient Beauty hath consented to be bound with chains that mankind may be released from its bondage, and hath accepted to be made a prisoner within this most mighty Stronghold that the whole world may attain unto true liberty."* Then, as I humbled myself and knelt before the Sacred Threshold of Bahá'u'lláh, my forehead touched a pure white cloth, upon which were scattered crimson rose petals, and a silence from the white heat of God's Face enwrapped me in a certitude

Outside of time, the soul's hangout, I took in knowing, God has no face. I took in white plaster walls, silent lacy ferns yearning their way up to pristine skylight. I took in the pilgrims' stocking feet from Turkey, Peru, Canada, China, feet carrying the beseeching heart for mankind's ordered life to be revolutionized, galvanized into an everlasting peace and the beginning of the advent of Divine Justice.

Around the world, some of the leaders played, hurling rocks and phrases suggesting "my testosterone is bigger than yours." For a time—nine days, to be exact—I listened to my footsteps across lightly molded curved pebbles, witnessing sounds of my feet across broken tiles, calling to mind brutalities of leaders gone by and empires stopped. Majesty was stamped on gardens on Mt. Carmel, every leaf, every mineral

---

* Bahá'í Writings.

opening up to serve the blessed feet of the ordinary in humanity who will come together no matter what. No boys-will-be-boys machinations can stop this quiet, soundless step towards our oneness.

Besides the white heat from the Face of God, bleaching my bones towards selflessness and service, a promise is made, viewed, and the silence shouts, over 'Akká "the silver city" and to Mount Carmel, the "Mountain of God," Isaiah's call: "Get thee up into the high mountain, O Zion that brightest good tidings," and David in his Psalms predicted, "Lift up your heads, O ye gates...the King of Glory shall come in," and I call to mind whilst standing in thick dimensions of purity the words uttered to an esteemed Orientalist of the time, Professor E.G. Browne. The words are from Bahá'u'lláh, Prophet-Founder of the Bahá'í Faith, offering words of light as beacons of hope, "These fruitless strifes, these ruinous wars shall pass away and the 'Most Great Peace' shall come."

Halo Moon Meets HyperPhysics over Falafel at the Mercaz

I sit here at the top of Mercaz in Israel, in a small, dart-in, take-a-quick-glance-to-the-left at a glass counter, a man stuffing a half pita with round crusty balls, and a cabinet filled with icy drinks, Coke being my falafel companion.

There's no halo moon sitting inside beside me on my chair, my Pilgrimage badge tucked into a pocket, so maybe baby I won't get overcharged as an innocent on her search for the proper chickpeas—big round ones, resting on a bed of hummus, surrounded by lettuce and pickles and cabbage and onions and tomatoes like it's the best Our Gang pita to hang out in.

Are you with me? How about these hills of Haifa? Yeah, I'm a newly-emerged mountain goat who just hoofed and cavorted her pilgrim heart right up to the Mercaz to shop, to wolf down a falafel, and to remember the other day when a friend and I were here, and to find a few gifts to take home.

Pilgrimage is not always about whispering of the "Face of God," which if you want to know, believe me, I'm not kidding, I found a phrase of that exact saying in a book I read today. Yesterday I said in my small writing, "There is no Face of God." Well, if I'm lying, I'm dying; there in that red-crimsoned covered book about Baha'u'llah, it referred in small black ink to "Face of God." This phrase has been used on a title of a book, but in my book the phrase referred to a title used for the Manifestations, Prophets, Messengers, and Divine Educators of God, so I am not just whistling Dixie when I tell you, "Boy, was I surprised."

But, hey, back to the falafel and me and relationships. Someone mentioned a Halo Moon, and I Googled it, because I have empty spaces in that vat of a brain of mine that resemble someone who had half a head severed like logs going into big blades, and the part that was severed for me was math, science, biology, stuff with details and makes me wonder, "Why did I only see my eyelashes in the microscope?"

Are you with me? So before I sit down and feel the hot crunch of chickpeas in the back of my throat, I am going to tell you this: I found on Google a term, HyperPhysics. Yes, I know some people play Solitaire on line, but me, I get lost in investigatory scientific hallways. As a writer with a strong poetic streak, I try to connect all my words, images and feelings into a HyperPhysics mode where everything is interconnected.

So I say, I'm going to connect a Halo Moon, as I feel pretty stuffed and fortified right now. That coke and falafel hit the spot and make me feel round and as if I'm producing extra circular rays of satisfaction around my round spots, just like a Halo Moon.

I'm going to tell you this hoofer has been praying her brains out (well parts anyhow) for Peace. It has been promised. Now don't give me any half-hearted reply or responses that peace isn't possible. If you do that, you've just been listening to all those boys at play on the planet who want parades and neon signs and national anthems and bling, lots of bling, so they won't think of the real stuff that matters, like the soul and its journey either to falafels or Hallowed White Spots.

Do you really think people, all of us on Planet Earth, can actually be stopped in our coming together, our HyperPhysics dance of oneness, because aren't we about creating an ever-advancing civilization?

Are you with me?

We All Fall Down

Destined lightness of being, sometimes
a danger in the urban world,
or planet of intrigue, politics, economic
need where gargoyles fly at night,
and things go bumpity bump.

It's a dance isn't it?
Living on the planet, one gone
tilt where we all fall down,
and yet, century after century
we get up.
After the Fall.

Yeah, after the Fall it's not
Original Sin anymore babe.
It's lightness of being,
inherent nobility
where falling is just another word
for glide patterns in the air.

Witness

Lord knows she tried when the blank paper was naked.

Open, receptive, until she scarred its blankness with angry reds, sorrowing blacks.

No witness to image and moment, so sacred the reader would gasp and carry on, despite a world of cruelty where CEO's get the protagonist's role in Dickens' *A Christmas Tale*.

No, she tried to capture years of bewilderment, male disdain: "No voice, you have no right. No voice, no voice, no voice."

But she saw moments pure like chaste whiteness of paper before the poem. What was one to do? No poem wrecker she—who wanted words to scruff and plump the soul—no minimalist pleasure, no aim for verisimilitude's false posture.

Then a tear fell upon the poem's page, and slowly luminescent silver formed a Lilliputian bell, a microcosm of chrysolite in Heaven's chapbook, the soul's recorder, and now "To Hurt the Poem" is to never speak, to keep silent the moments of this age.

Taking the Voice for a Walk
(Spring, 2005)

Now, sweet now, an atavistic run at sibilants, bilabial plosives and fricatives, all entombed under the dome of my pointed head in a place now known as publisher of *Ploughshares*, but to my skinny, cigarette-smoking '50s pony-tailed self was Emerson College, holed up on Beacon Street, home of hippies, broadcasting wannabees; some good actors, and a man named Ken, whose crutches clanked through the hallways with vestiges of polio's memory wrapping around his twitching, rabbit-thin calves. Ken, on the stage, crawled out of a ravaged body to mesmerize and to make verisimilitude soup as he played Eliza Doolittle.

Now my mouth, frozen, carping, sad, whining, complaining, must abandon its round o's, the o's of a '50s cigarette smoker, blowing smoke rings into the open sky, because today, amidst tall buildings, near Coffee Bean wheels and deals, I sit in a squatty building which mirrors my squatty and satisfied heart. I hit sounding sounds, twisting, mouthy phrases, as I feel motion, and tongue my ponderous one-and-only back tooth.

I call to mind dentists of the past, dentists of the '50s. Visualize aluminum, or *aluminium*, if you like Alistair Cooke's way of speaking trippingly on the tongue. Solipsism's memory serves up a time of aluminum fillings and small hands—mine—gripping the dentist's chair; because Novocain, an indulgence of the highest order, and of me, always in dentist chairs of well-heeled men of Tufts and USC fame, who smile clinically at me, click figures in their heads, and calibrate higher learning fees for a daughter's study in Museum Mold.

My mouth breaks out, parses sounds from pursed lips: "Prunes are good for you," as I remember Emerson College classes, speech classes, and my timidity, ribboning itself from socks and loafers on up to a tightened throat. No right to speak. In real life, whatever that ephemeral term means, I mumble, because of fatigue, laziness, capped teeth over a fractured root. I can give devotion to detail new meaning when I talk about my teeth—for that matter, my body. Where does one start? Four-pound baby, being a twin, serious illness at six months, early childhood illness, car accidents, and a plastic aortic valve named after a Catholic saint? Still, whining and moaning will not do. Why I mumble I don't know.

When I do readings, my words are clear and focused. My lips tenderly touch a bilabial *p*. My teeth and mouth feel the tickle of an outgoing *f*; or how about VR of Vroman's Bookstore in Pasadena, creating a mild Santa Ana wind through my half opened lips. Finally, it appears, a resultant widening of a mouth interminably small. I discover a calisthenics class for the couch-potato mouth, like one probably held elsewhere, like Westwood or Vista Del Mar. I sign up to feel the stretch to both sides of a wall as I pronounce, "the sea ceaseth and sufficeth us," and think of a warm body of a whale slobbering next to me eating all the Twinkies.

It's all about being mouthy. Yeah, speaking up.

For me.

Yeah.

For others.

Yeah.

I can deal.

Why I Write

Like now, when the dishes sit orphaned in the kitchen sink because I, their washer, am out clicking away at my keyboard, typing, sharing, breathing, living, putting off the inevitable. Because once a long time ago, I was so hurt I couldn't breathe. I carried an intake of hurt with me forever, until I found out that sensitivity is the price and the prize in order to become a hollow reed for others.

I write for myself. I write for others. I write to others. I write to a woman in Chowchilla, falsely imprisoned for defending herself against her rapist and abusive stepfather. She tells me she liked the phrase in an essay of mine: "The language of God is a tear running down someone's cheek."

I write because I read insatiably, gobbling, inhaling, filling myself with the human condition. Some days, I am splat on the floor like a big old squished bug, its body swept up by old straws on a broom. Other days, I write to show my younger view of the magic of St. Theresa's Snow Queen Altar when I was seven, when everything looked like a wedding cake.

When I was younger, I was terrifically needy. I could have impaled myself on a stake wide and big, sort of like a meta-letter holder, and I could have run this huge pole right through my insatiable heart, with a note on my back: "Loves too much." I write because I have gone beyond Medieval Posts puncturing despair and loneliness and have decided maybe men love too much or we all love too much or too little.

We are told by images in advertising that we should be thin, jaded, look like models for glossy fashion magazines, whose eyes suggest an ability to shoot up on a lunch hour. Despair is trendy. Nihilism and materialism and not giving a damn might be the language of the hour.

But out in the world of readers and would-be writers and writers, some lonely, little, big, young, old, trembling, brassy, you catch-my-drift writer, writes because he or she must. Words have a visceral effect upon her, him, the dog, the surrounding room, hopes for the world, and maybe a good ham sandwich (or description thereof) on a sour dough roll, with slabs of mayo, and a bed of lettuce.

You know, what this nation needs is a good ham sandwich and a Pepsi without the Aspartame and some honest-to-goodness dealing with truth. Hey, maybe it's okay to love and not love, to fear and not fear. Let's be real, be afraid of bugs in knotty pine walls when the walls come alive at night.

At this moment, I watch an elderly blind woman clutch the corners of her walker, take a breath, and remain a sweet, sweet spirit. She thinks her tests are of the divinely calibrated kind, even though metaphoric trucks have run over her.

I write to honor her, to speak of the anonymous amongst us. I love to watch bravery in action and small acts of courage, and what about kindness in our nation while the world is narcissistically checking its derriere in the mirror?

Does anyone listen to the intake of breath at midnight as the poor contemplate a way out? I write to speak and suggest we must have immense courage and speak up. We gotta talk, yeah, walk the talk, and we must share our hopes for a future where humankind will live in harmony and prosperity.

I suggest someday we will all be sensitive, spiritually inclined, and aware of our oneness. The sense of "the other" will go on a back shelf, like Twinkies, no longer approved of by the American Heart Association. Maybe writing will be celebrated by hoots and hollers and a piping or two from a medieval horn or Siberian throat.

I hope the arts will have a way of grabbing our souls' innards and carrying us through the day. These are some of the reasons I write, but there are others. Today is Wednesday, and these are my Wednesday writing reasons.

Beyond the Fringe

So get this. It's hot and I'm drinking my second cup of coffee, and the phone rings. It's the lab, and my blood is too thin. You tell me what I should say. So I tell the lab people, "Look I work out, but it gets hot, and I didn't tell them I do the sauna too. They should catch my drift. Hot is hot. Sauna is also a street in Texas where I recently spent 20 minutes. So I tell the lady, "Yes." I listen to her directions and "Yes, I won't take Coumadin tonight." We hang up. I wanted to tell her, get this, "Didja know Coumadin is really rat poison, and didja know that, and get this, Emma Bovary died of an overdose of rat poison?"

I tell you urban living; so I agreed, "Yeah I'll go in next week for another test." Then my day takes another twist. I decide I can't risk working out. Workouts scare me at times, so Bill says, "I'll go for a walk with you," and honestly, I mean to walk. I get on these weird rubber-with-holes-in-them shoes, put my backpack on, and hit the driveway, and get halfway down to the driveway to the mail slot and feel weak and decide, "Nope, no walking for me."

So then Bill and I look at each other and decide to go to Ralph's and get our groceries, but then, it's still hot, so we think is Donna at her restaurant? Donna is someone I told to go to Jack Grapes for his writing workshop because she's a standup comic. So we head for Donna's restaurant because we are devotees. I search the menu for cabbage dishes, because Vitamin K in cabbage thickens my blood. It's not like the plot thickens, honestly that's literary, and this is real; close to the body; my blood. I remember Julie, the healer, telling me, "You are way up there on the Richter scale," and get this, I laughed. I don't know why I spin off and think I should just laugh, because I'm scared at times. I order a panini with spinach in it and cabbage salad on the side.

We meet a bunch of people; guys next to us who work on the Spitzer telescope at Cal Tech when they aren't hanging at Donna's. The Spitzer takes pics of Mars or Earth; and funny jokes come out with these guys and Donna. Donna tells us of her new business venture in two years; and we are right behind her.

So then Bill and I eat lunch and head off towards Ralph's as the heat swims clear off the sidewalk. I go in first to hit the air-conditioned store and head for the cabbage and broccoli. Broccoli, lasts longer, and I can steam it and put light mayo and Tamari sauce on it. Get this - it's to die for; yes to die for, but it's not for me to die but to keep me alive and staying within the American Heart Association guidelines.

We buy pomegranate juice, the kind that comes in a curved and indented bottle to make it look like Nirvana Juice. It's good with sparkling water, and then whaddya know when we leave Ralphs, the sky is overcast. We feel as if we're walking through powdered heat; like snow when there's a blizzard, but the heat feels like a hedge from the ground to the sky. I want to go home and just crash, and we do so until Johnnie comes by to do grammar stuff out of his Kaplan book. I was an English major, but not the anal retentive kind, but I am taught as a kid to speak the King's English. Get this. If you pronounce your ings and speak good English and never say swear words, my family of origin promises me a wonderfully successful life where doors open miraculously all because of the dulcet tones of my King's English. So in my second marriage, which is wonderful, I marry a guy who butchers the language but is a math brain and an ardent funny soul, and he did better economically than I in the earlier years.

Get this; it doesn't matter now. We are in this together and basically live what I would call beyond the fringe, which I think scares some people. I gotta tell you, though, inner worlds open up; blast you away to the worlds of the tilted sane and unusual, which reminds me of the people at the restaurant today told Donna, "We are from Pluto," and she said, "That works here."

That's our life; beyond the fringe, the alternative pathways route, and I think I celebrate them all. It's still hot; and I gotta go to the end of the driveway and meet Johnnie who's picking me up to go to fireside; and that's the facts, Jack.

Sometimes

Sometimes when I get mail, I remember the Million Dollar Man who isn't around anymore, not since Enron and all that stuff. Sometimes when I shop, I wonder how many people worry about the price of lettuce or economic shadows.

Sometimes when I walk past Lake Street shops, in Pasadena, I think who is going to buy all this stuff? Sometimes when I fold up inside like a cheap, heavy green army tent, I go for a walk instead.

Sometimes when the phone rings, I think of the telemarketer being someone's kid; learning at 19 to control pimples, money worries, and where and how to fit in this tightly tracked existence where it helps to go to Harvard, but not necessarily with big student loans.

Sometimes when a winter day goes too soon into that five o'clock dark, I remember being a little girl with braids, on Wren Street, looking up at an old fashioned lamppost which had just clicked on and asking God to make sure I got married.

And sometimes, now that I'm married to a very good guy for 24 years, I think: smart lamppost! Thanks, God.

Writer's Block

I am a limp noodle slithering along pale sidewalks pretending I am a worm, and worms don't write, which is good. I just can be a slitherer because the heat has knocked me out, plus nose biopsy and leg biopsy. Nothing big has happened, but I can't stop bleeding drip by drip, which seems a perfect excuse for writer's block.

Today I write to the end of the line of paper which is white and blank, and I feel that you—forget you—I have to be willing to go to the end of the line and face the unknown spots and places and all the while galvanize myself into action. A mere walking into blank space, that's really what we do. We walk in blank space—heavenly.

Mercury Rises

"See you around the bend, "I say,
wondering what talisman
presents itself: an eagle amongst
dappled clouds, while
a lone deer views me,
not afraid to keep
her brown eyes on my face
steady as she goes.

Me and my shadow do our oneness
walk, like twins, but more than
twinning as shadows lie in
oceanic lands of Lilliputians, Goths and
20th Century Models with
slashed red mouths and jutting cheek bones,
eyes of whom are hollow, don't you know,
to reflect the age we think we live in.

But we can count on the fact that
Mercury rises and Divine Mercy may
accompany our peripatetic Mercury, often
Tongue in Cheek, and now with shadows
dancing, they inform us of light
and darkness' Dance of Promise.

Writing Weakness

I don't like to be crass. That's my writing weakness. I never ever write about sexuality. Yet there lurks an adolescent side of me, who remembers laughing inappropriately and uncontrollably as a teenager when titles of books were the rage: A Broken Bra Strap by Wan Hung Lo; or songs, "After dark we'll take a walk and goose the statues in the park." Don't forget love scenes, when for years I referred to the upper portion of my body as "my chest," and "down there" reminded me of Gilda Radner's skit where her mom tells her, "Gilda, some day you will want to use the lower portion of your body."

So it goes. I like love scenes, as in Gloria Naylor's *Women of Brewster Place*, where she describes lovemaking as wandering through all fields and myriad prisms of color; and the graphic stuff like Henry Miller language, not to be mentioned, isn't put in. Years ago I read *Lady Chatterley's Lover* and loved it. I am no longer interested in the engineering aspects of writing about lovemaking, but feel the beauty of the whole thing is private. So the stuff I write mixes the spiritual with the real.

Take the eff-word. For years I used it because I didn't drink, smoke, take drugs, gossip, blah, blah. Instead I swore like a trucker pulling out of Tarzana into a traffic snarl. It doesn't add to the text. At times it might. Language has to be carefully used. That's why I like Raymond Carver, who deals with the dry underbelly of neurosis and psychosis in a minimalist way. When his words and sentences walk across the page, there's background noise of a cool, freeway wind tunneling alongside his passages, wrapping his prose in an existential hollowness.

For years I didn't write dialogue. My first short story was about a dog and his mistress. The dog only spoke using inner thoughts. The very idea of three people in a short story speaking to one another and moving them around a couch made me collapse in a heap. One of my writing weaknesses is overwriting. "We all have some writing weakness," a teacher told me. I also hate beach books and romances and stuff like that. I am a memoir maven, and Pasadena Central Library categorizes memoir under 092 (actually it is 92, short for 920–biography; 092 is the Dewey classification for "Block Books"). I am a homing pigeon by the 092s marked "new" in that wonderful big wood paneled Central Library. But speaking of romance again, I'm going to stop writing this for now and have a toasted tuna sandwich which my husband made for me as an act of high romance! I've become a lousy speller; it comes with brain fog—gratefully not Alzheimer's, but from mold spores that I still hold on to, but not intentionally.

About the Author

Esther Bradley-DeTally is the author of *Without A Net: A Sojourn in Russia.* She has published various essays and poetry in numerous publications such as *Orison, Herald of the South, On the Bus, M0th, Equal Circles,* and *The Trees Clapped Their Hands.* She lives in Pasadena with her husband and imaginary pug dog.

www.ingramcontent.com/pod-product-compliance
Ingram Content Group UK Ltd.
Pitfield, Milton Keynes, MK11 3LW, UK
UKHW041958230426
12048UKWH00008B/395